The approach to Johnstown's Inclined Plane, the
steepest funicular inclined plane in the world.

Dawn rising behind the mountains to the east,
brightening the sky over Market Street.

*The early morning sun casting reflections on the
windows of Vine Street buildings.*

The First Lutheran Church as seen
against the foliage of distant hills.

THE TRIUMPH OF THE AMERICAN SPIRIT

Johnstown, Pennsylvania

Preface by
LEE IACOCCA

Text by
HOWARD MUSON

Principal Photography by
DAVID FINN
AMY BINDER

Published by the Johnstown Flood Museum and

The American Association for State and Local History Library
Lanham • New York • London

DESIGNER: ULRICH RUCHTI
ASSOCIATE DESIGNER: MICHAEL SCHUBERT

Copyright © 1989 by the American Association for State and
Local History Library, A Division of University Publishing
Associates, Inc.

4720 Boston Way
Lanham, Maryland 20706

3 Henrietta Street
London WC2E 8LU England

Printed in the United States of America

British Cataloging-in-Publication Information Available

Co-published by arrangement with
The Johnstown Flood Museum

Library of Congress Cataloging-in-Publication Data

Muson, Howard.
   Triumph of the American spirit Johnstown,
Pennsylvania.

   1. Johnstown (Pa.)—History.   2. Johnstown
(Pa.)—Description—View.   3. Johnstown (Pa.)
—Economic conditions.   4. Floods—Pennsylvania
—Johnstown—History—19th century.   I. Title.
F159.J7M87   1989   974.8'77   89-291
ISBN 0-8026-0032-8 (alk. paper)

All AASLH LIBRARY books are produced on acid-free paper which
exceeds the minimum standards set by the National Historical
Publications and Records Commission.

Supported by a grant from the National Park
Service, U.S. Department of the Interior.

CONTENTS

PREFACE

Johnstown has a great story to tell, and I'm glad it's being told to the rest of the country through this book.

There is probably no place in America that has gone through what the people of Johnstown have: three disastrous floods, its major industries on the ropes, for many years the highest unemployment rate in the nation.

Johnstown has put the tough times behind it, and I know a sense of humor must have helped. This book is part of the centennial of the Great Johnstown Flood. Who ever heard of a centennial of a flood! They didn't even do one for Noah!

But Johnstown is proud of the special spirit of its people. The industrial heritage project that Johnstown has underway tells what made this city—and this country—great in the first place. It tells how all the Italians and the Slavs and the others came to Johnstown and built the steel mills and dug the coal. My father was one of them, which is why I feel so close to this part of the country. Arriving from Italy in 1902 at the age of 12, he had a tag around his neck, and somehow was sent to western Pennsylvania to work in the coal mines. He lasted one day, after which he ran away to Allentown, and that's where I was born and raised. If he had gone in a slightly different direction, I would have been a Johnstowner.

Maybe one of the most surprising things about Johnstown is that its population has remained steady over the years. It was under water in 1977, and just about the time it dried out the steel industry was hit by tough competition from overseas. And yet the people of Johnstown didn't pack up and move to Houston, like so many others did a few years ago. They didn't abandon their homes. They stayed and adjusted and rebuilt. And now Johnstown is listed as one of the top twenty cities to live in the United States!

Some say that we Americans have somehow gotten soft and a little lazy and lost our will to compete. The story of Johnstown and its people proves it isn't so. It's a story of courage, and determination and pride. And it's a lesson for all Americans.

Lee A. Iacocca

*The City of Johnstown spread out in
the valley—a view from the top of the
Inclined Plane.*

INTRODUCTION

On an afternoon in late summer, looking out from the observation deck atop Westmont hill, the small American city below appears almost preserved in amber. Sounds of activity at this height are dull echoes. The air is still. The mind fills with haunting images of the past. About 500 feet below, the city of Johnstown, Pennsylvania, is spread out on the valley floor amid its amphitheater of rolling green hills.

From this vantage point, which visitors can reach by taking a rail lift called the Inclined Plane or a steep, winding road, the eye takes in the sweeping vista of a former mill town that is on its way to becoming something else. The city is snugly situated at the bottom of a bowl in the Allegheny Mountains, about 78 miles east of Pittsburgh. Pleasant buildings of brick and stone, none more than a few stories high—banks, hospitals, a Holiday Inn, a glass transportation center—rise from its central grid of streets. Two rivers meet in its midst to form a third, the Conemaugh, which flows westward out of the valley. The long sheds and stacks of a steel works are clustered along the river banks like rows of tiny wood factories in a business board game. A stone railroad bridge crosses the Conemaugh down below; a small steel bridge spans the river entering the valley from the east. At the confluence of the three rivers, known as the Point, there is a fair-sized stadium and a small park.

This valley, with its intensive concentration of natural resources—

water, coal, iron, limestone—was one of the birthplaces of industrial America, an important link in the westward expansion of the country. In the second half of the 19th century, the valley gave birth to what the *New York Times* called "the finest iron works in the country and one of the glories of Pennsylvania industry." The Cambria Iron Company, later the Cambria Steel Company, was a major producer of rails for the railroads as they advanced across the continent and a leading innovator in iron- and steelmaking techniques. Its long arms reached into the surrounding countryside to scoop up vast resources, and into the lives of the thousands who toiled in its various enterprises. In a 1940 Ph.D. thesis written at the University of Pittsburgh, Nathan Daniel Shappee described the Cambria Iron Works at the height of its power:

"When the traveler crossed the stone bridge, the greatest view of the works was on the left. Four blast furnaces roared night and day. The boom of the rolling mill pounded against his ears. Showers of sparks created the only beauty of the scene. Bessemer retorts grumbled into an angry roar as they spit out the impurities of molten metal in their hot mouths. Turning from this scene of noise and smoke and frightening fire, the visitor could see cattle grazing on the company's farms in the surrounding hills—a strange contrast to the hot, dirty confusion nearer at hand. When his train left Johnstown station for the trip over the mountains, the visitor's view of Johnstown was hidden by the passing of freight and ore trains bound for the mills. The loads in the cars came from the company's own ore fields—spiegeleizen and fossil ores from Frankstown, levant ore from Marklesburg, soft and hard fossil ores from Hopewell, hematite from Huntingdon County, limonite from Springfield and manganiferous ores from Henrietta."

Charles Schwab, one of the titans of the steel industry in this century, grew up in Loretta, Pennsylvania, 20 miles away. He once recalled the view of Johnstown that he saw on his visits to the city:

"Along toward dusk tongues of flame would shoot up in the pall around Johnstown. When some furnace door was opened the evening turned red. A boy watching from the rim of hills had a vast arena before him, a place of vague forms, great labors, and dancing fires. It gets into your hair, your clothes, even your blood."

The skies over Johnstown no longer glow red in the evenings. The smells and particulates are gone from the air. The Bethlehem Steel Corporation, which has owned the Cambria Works since 1923, shut down many of its operations in Johnstown during the steel slump of the 1970s and early 1980s; it is, however, betting heavily on a turnaround in a few modernized plants left in the city. Once some 70 percent of the area's blue-collar workers were employed in the mills and coal mines. Today Johnstown is no longer a one-company steel town. The city of 32,000 serves as a hub to 18 other municipalities, with a total population of about 93,000 in the city area. Most of the borough of Johnstown's jobs are now in services—in three major hospitals, in utility and construction companies that maintain headquarters there, in 10 banks and in retail businesses.

Because of its relative isolation in a narrow valley, Johnstown has the look and feel of a small town. This is a city of manageable size, about 4½ miles long, of human proportions. A brisk walker can go from one end of the downtown to the other in fewer than 10 minutes. It is a friendly, easygoing place where people stop and chat on the street and may even address a casual comment to a total stranger.

On a summer's day in the downtown, the green hills loom everywhere around. The wide sidewalks of Main Street are inlaid with brick and look freshly cemented. Buildings from a variety of historical periods, decorated with American flags, face onto beautiful Central Park with its sparkling fountain and gardens. The people who come and go on the park benches are casually dressed, the men, typically, in baseball caps; many look like retirees. The only reminder that this is a mill town is when the Gautier

The United States Post Office Building in Johnstown,
built 1912–1914 in the Greek Revival Commercial
style, represents the optimism felt about Johnstown in
the first decade of the 20th century. This building
became the Crown American Corporation
office in 1968.

Lee Hospital, a fine medical facility
serving residents of two counties.

*Central Park at midday, when friends
can enjoy a few moments of pleasant
relaxation.*

Wire Works at the end of Clinton Street hoves into view.

Much has been written about early capitalism in America, the generation of Carnegies, Rockefellers and Fords, and the coming of manufacturing to America's rural communities. Main Street and Middletown, U.S.A., have had their share of chroniclers and corner-store sociologists. But the mill towns have been curiously overlooked in the literature. Mark Reutter, a journalist, observes in a recent book about the Bethlehem works at Sparrows Point in Baltimore:

"Located on the fringe of metropolitan areas or in small cities, the mill capitals of America were imprisoned in their own blankets of soot and corporate control—they were the ash heaps that Gatsby and Daisy rushed by with eyes averted. Reports on the steel trade concentrated on corporate headquarters, not on the night-and-day blazings of Johnstown, Pennsylvania; Weirton, West Virginia; Gary, Indiana, or Youngstown, Ohio."

Johnstown did blaze across the front pages of the nation's newspapers for one tragic moment in its history, during the Great Johnstown Flood of 1889. More than 2,200 people died in that disaster, caused by the collapse of a dam in the mountains to the northeast after two days of heavy rains.

In the past 100 years the people of this small southwestern Pennsylvania city have been hit by two more major floods and a few minor ones. They have responded to these disasters with a characteristic tenacity and good humor. Ask them why they stay in a place that has been wiped out by three major floods in the last century and they may chuckle and answer, "Don't know—guess we're either hardy people or just too dumb to leave!"

The remark is heard so often one suspects it is the stock reply to curious visitors. But they *are* hardy, and there is nothing defensive in the comment at all. Though Johnstown has been known since 1889 as the Flood City, though it has been portrayed in two movies filmed there as a typical depressed steel town (*Slap Shot* and *All the Right Moves*), the people are not ashamed of their town. In fact, they'd sooner move to Mars than

*Stark and dramatic cylindrical
ventilators dot rooftops of Johnstown's
steel factories. These are seen above the
Gautier Division of Bethlehem Steel.*

pull up their roots in Johnstown—a fairly astonishing sentiment given the restless ebb and flow of other Americans. Whatever it is that keeps them there—family, a shared sense of their history, distance from the problems of larger urban areas—the residents of this valley and neighboring towns like to stay put. The visitor to Johnstown will hear countless stories about all those who left for a time and later came back to live.

The Great Flood of 1889 was an event of Biblical proportions that turned into a national spectacle. But it is now far from the minds of Johnstowners, a poignant but distant memory of a tragedy suffered by the quaint people of another century. Johnstowners today probably have little to fear from floods, although the 1977 disaster is still fresh in memory and, as we shall see, they have learned not to get too confident when it comes to their safety.

In 1989, Johnstowners planned to commemorate the 100th anniversary of the Great Flood with a series of events from late spring to fall. They were, of course, not celebrating a flood but their heritage, their resilience. After each disaster, they have built and rebuilt their city. In doing it, they have learned valuable lessons. Each time they have mobilized to get outside help, bringing massive new infusions of capital to revitalize business—in effect, an urban renewal program in every generation. They have learned game-saving plays, what one writer called "creative community strategies."

The best qualities of the American character are as abundantly evident in the city's past as the thick iron and coal seams that run beneath the hills. The pioneer's will to subdue the forces of nature, the immigrant's strong work ethic and determination to survive, the ingenuity and craftsmanship of a nation of builders, the strength that Tocqueville saw in the power of free men to associate to achieve common ends: These themes are all present in Johnstown, magnified and clarified by the people's responses to tragedy—a triumph of the American spirit.

A plaque on the wall of the American House identifies it as an historic building that survived the 1889 flood.

The Stone Bridge casts its reflection on the now
quiet waters of the Conemaugh River which on
May 31, 1889, was a raging torrent.

*Striking architecture in a beautifully landscaped
environment gives a distinctive character to the
Johnstown campus of the University of
Pittsburgh.*

The glass panels of the Main Street
East Complex reflect the cloud patterns
of the sky above, giving downtown
Johnstown a look of the future.

A sculptured elk peers at the neighboring hills
while standing on its perch atop the Johnstown
Elks Lodge.

Built just after the 1889 flood, the decorative facade of Main Street's Dibert building is an impressive example of late nineteenth-century architecture.

The cataclysmic horror of the great flood, as portrayed in an illustration from Harper's Weekly printed in 1889 one week after the flood.

*A statue of "Morley's Dog," a mythical saver of
lives during the flood, stands across the way from
City Hall, ironically protected by a sign stating
"No Dogs Allowed." In actuality this artifact of
the 1889 flood was a lawn ornament.*

"I was always proud that I came from Johnstown," says Frances Hesselbein, the national executive director of the Girl Scouts of the U.S.A., who traces her lineage in the area back to the Revolutionary War. "Johnstown is a city of survivors. Whether it is a natural catastrophe or industrial and economic problems, Johnstowners find ways to cope. And they do more than cope, they move forward. There is a sense of renewal there."

The photographs and text that follow will convey a sense of how it has gone for Johnstown in the past 100 years. The words and pictures add up to an essay on one of America's greatest mill towns, the ethnic peoples who came together there, their skills, their sacrifices, their daily lives. It is the story of a town that was long under the domination of a single enterprise and has now begun to emerge with larger sense of itself, a community of builders and rebuilders who are struggling to adapt to the economic changes beyond the hills while hanging onto the values that have sustained them until now.

High water marks on a corner of City Hall, showing the levels reached in each of Johnstown's three floods.

BUILDERS AND
REBUILDERS

Walking the tree-lined streets of Johnstown, the visitor bumps into history on every corner. The former Franklin Street Methodist Church that parted the enormous wave sweeping through Johnstown during the '89 flood still stands. The rough beige stone of the municipal building has markings showing the levels reached by the flood waters in 1889, 1936, and 1977. All over the city the eye alights on fine architectural details and oddities—the carved designs on Victorian storefronts, the Art Deco entrance to the telephone company building, the small elk statue atop the Elks Lodge.

In the early morning, the few people in the streets are workmen, building, cleaning, repairing, painting. There is an amazing energy in the quiet valley. In Central Park, a young man on a ladder is putting a fresh coat of gold paint on a bust statue of the city's founder, a Pennsylvania German immigrant named Joseph Johns. At the intersection of Vine and Franklin streets, near the steel bridge, workers are completing a palatial new headquarters for the Crown America Corporation, a developer of shopping malls and hotels. Designed by one of America's leading architects, Michael Graves, the structure features a facade of rose and gray-blue stone topped by a neoclassical colonnade.

The most ubiquitous feature of Johnstown's skyline is its churches.

No fewer than 72 of them are packed into this area of some five square miles. Gothic spires, bell towers and the onion domes of Eastern Orthodox churches rise everywhere from the downtown streets and the surrounding hills. Many of these churches are quite beautiful, with exquisite stained glass, frescoes and carved doors, attesting to the power of religion in the lives of the city's diverse ethnic communities.

George D. Zamias sits at his desk in his spacious office on Market Street in Johnstown surrounded by the furniture and people in his life—an antique globe, pictures of his family, his diploma from the Joseph Johns Junior High School, a picture of his company's 12-passenger Merlin 4C airplane. In one corner, set in Italian marble, is an old shoeshine stand of polished brass. "He stays in practice in case business goes bad," says his wife, Marianna, seated at a conference table a few feet from his desk.

Zamias is one of two developers in Johnstown who have become wealthy building shopping malls around the country. The other is Frank Pasquerilla, chief executive of the Crown America Corporation. Both typify the qualities from which many in Johnstown draw strength: gratitude for the courage and sacrifices of immigrant parents, high energy, zest for work, love of family and community.

The tanned, 58-year-old Zamias spends much of his time flying to other cities to look over sites, but he is always relieved to return to Johnstown, where he was raised and where his father, a Greek immigrant from the island of Kos, owned a shoeshine and hat-cleaning parlor right around the corner on Main Street.

"I must have shined a million pairs of shoes," Zamias says. "What's helped me tremendously is the work ethic my father taught me." While growing up, he and his four brothers worked eight to ten hours a day in their father's shop; the family lived on the top floor of the three-story building facing the city's Central Park. They put their substantial tips in a bank and built up a savings. "You know, we never went anywhere," he recalls.

Zamias, who earned all A's at Johnstown High School and was vale-dictorian of his graduating class, taught business courses at the University of Pittsburgh for a while and was just a few credits short of earning a Ph.D. before going into business. Today his company employs about 70 people in Johnstown and more than 300 in branch offices. His wife and three of his four sons also work in the business.

Almost everything in the company's office was lost in the 1977 flood, but Zamias went about the painstaking task of replacing it. So deep are Zamias' roots in the downtown (his office was actually built on the site where his junior high once stood) that the thought of moving his head-quarters to higher ground never crossed his mind.

When asked why he loves Johnstown, George Zamias unabashedly lists all the homely virtues that used to keep people in small towns–"You get to know everybody, and everybody gets to know you on a first-name basis; you have rapport with your neighbors." Zamias adds: "I've been in all the major cities, and you couldn't get me to live in any of them. The traffic alone would drive me batty. I can't wait till I get in and out of the big towns. That's why I've concentrated most of my malls in the middle markets such as the Johnstowns, the Altoonas, the Meadvilles, the Wilkes-Barres."

Frank Pasquerilla has shown similar gratitude to the city in which he was raised. A native of the city's Woodvale section, he was headed for college when his father's fatal illness, blacklung disease, altered his plans. He joined a fledgling masonry company, Crown Construction, in 1951 as a payroll clerk and junior engineer. By 1956 he was president of the company. In 1961 he became its sole owner.

A billion-dollar corporation today, Crown American employs 200 people locally and controls 32 million square feet of property in malls, shopping centers, hotels, and department stores in ten states. Cited by Monitor magazine in 1988 as the nation's fastest growing development

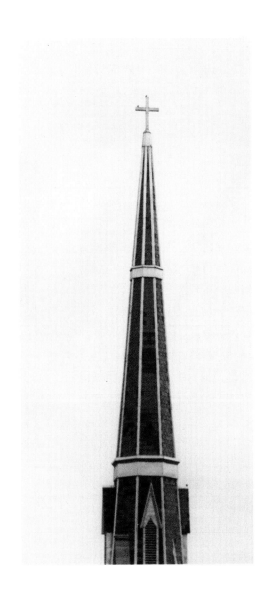

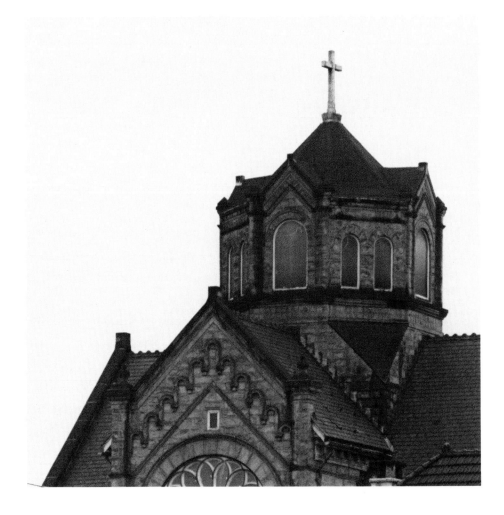

*Johnstown is a city of churches
with a spiritual heritage which
can be seen in the steeples,
towers and religious figures
which reach into the sky.
Clockwise from the far left:
The Franklin Street United
Methodist Church;
St. Stephen's Church;
Statue of Mary and Jesus from
St. John Gualbert Cathedral;
Bell Tower, St. John
Gualbert; St. Joseph's,
Railroad Street;
St. Casimir's Church.*

35

A parade in downtown Johnstown marks the
city's 100th anniversary in 1900.

company, Crown American remains based in Johnstown. "We've had a lot of opportunities to move—to Pittsburgh, New York, Washington D.C.—but Johnstown is my home," Pasquerilla says. "I grew up here. My wife and family are here. The company grew up here, too."

That's why he's elected to build his company's $28 million headquarters in the downtown. The architect, Michael Graves, says that the developer wanted other companies to follow his example. In effect, they'll say, "If it's good enough for Pasquerilla to stay in town, we'll stay here, too, rather than going to the suburbs and building some nondescript glass box."

Graves credits the company for its commitment to an ambitious plan. "They wanted an architect who would give the building the attention that Frank Lloyd Wright gave to the Johnson & Johnson headquarters in Racine, Wisconsin," he says. They also wanted the employees to be enthusiastic about the ambiance. Graves says, "Most corporate offices do not describe the people who occupy them. The buildings don't make them feel comfortable about who they are and what the company does."

A central atrium welcomes visitors to the main entrance on Vine Street, while a second entrance with a port-cochere on Franklin Street gives employees easy street access. The colonnade that crowns the building hides the cooling towers and other apparatus, but, says Graves, is also a play on the corporate name. Though original and dramatic, the architecture blends admirably with the setting: the rough-hewn stone and pastel facade compliment the gray stone of the Gothic First Lutheran Church on Vine and the reddish-brown of the massive Romanesque First United Methodist Church across the street.

Johnstowners have been building and rebuilding for a hundred years, and there are many examples of such craftsmanship and attention to architectural detail around the city. On the Westmont heights, splendid homes in early Colonial Revival, Queen Anne and more modern styles line the quiet residential streets; many feature wraparound porches, gabled dormer windows, tall pillars, stained and beveled leaded-glass windows and carriage houses.

The suburb was built on land owned by the Cambria Iron Works after the '89 flood, as the people of the valley sought a safe refuge in the hills from future disasters. Charles R. Miller of Philadelphia, who planned the Philadelphia suburb of Bryn Mawr, was the designer of Westmont. He also designed Westmont's Grandview Cemetery, where there is a memorial to victims of the '89 flood and many rows of simple white slabs mark the graves of bodies that were never identified. The curvilinear design of Grandview is modeled after English cemeteries and offers sweeping vistas.

Originally, Westmont was roughly divided into separate neighborhoods, called "the dinner side" and "the supper side," as determined by the status and income of the residents. The company's elite and the town's richest merchants lived in the grandest homes on the dinner side, while foremen and some skilled workers built or rented on the supper side.

The suburb's most elegant street, the broad, elm-covered Luzerne, was created by Henry Rogers, the architect who designed more homes than any other in Westmont. Rogers came from Pittsburgh to live on Luzerne Street. One of his outstanding homes was built at 535 Tioga Street for Russell C. Love, owner of the Johnstown candy company, a massive residence with rustic stone and wood shingling, a wraparound porch supported by rough-hewn ashlar pillars and diamond-pattered lattice glass on the upper sashes. Another popular architect in Johnstown was Walter R. Myton of Huntingdon, Pennsylvania, who built the spacious residence at 434 Luzerne Street in Westmont that reflects the early influence of Frank Lloyd Wright.

At the time of the '89 flood, the city directory listed six firms under "builders and contractors." One of the best-remembered builders was the German-born Otto Scharmann, who after the flood reportedly had "more contracts than he could handle." According to a recent report of the Na-

Internationally renowned architect Michael
Graves has designed this new headquarters for
Crown American Corporation, one of
Johnstown's leading corporate enterprises.

*A neo-classical architectural element on
top of one of the belltowers of St. John
Gaulbert Church.*

tional Park Service, Scharmann's trademark was the ornate beveled-glass sidelights and transoms in many of Westmont's large old homes. One source of Johnstown's stained and art glass was the studio of William Heslop, established in 1888. The studio furnished the glass for churches as well as residences, and also made mirrors.

Johnstown's architecture reflects many outside influences. The will to build and rebuild, however, comes from its people and seems almost bred in the bone. Edward Joseph Cernik is another kind of Johnstown builder, a successful businessman who lost almost everything in the 1977 flood but hope and a fierce work ethic.

Cernik's father came to Johnstown from Bled in Yugoslavia, worked in a coal mine and then a steel mill, saving money in hopes of returning to Bled. He never went back. The father married and started a family; he invested his savings in an apartment house and remained in Johnstown all his life.

The son, after service in the Korean War, took courses in auto-body and electrical work at the Vale Technical Institute in Blairsville. During a 33-year career at Bethlehem Steel, Ed Cernik worked most of the time in a scarfing yard "using a big torch to take the defects out of finished steel." He arranged his shifts so that he could devote time to a garage for auto repairs that he and his wife built near their home in Tanneryville on the road leading northeast out of Johnstown. Before long, they had a second garage and gas station, then a dealership to sell Suzuki motorcycles. Cernik, his wife, and their three growing sons worked in their businesses, all in the same neighborhood a short walk from their front door. Ed Cernik's work week is seldom fewer than seven days long, though he retired from Bethlehem four years ago.

They lived in the shadow of a hill facing the Conemaugh River. When the rains came in July 1977—an incredible 12 inches fell that night—the Cerniks' businesses were all flooded. Water from overflowing creeks and

An especially attractive residential area,
Luzerne Street in Westmont, with its
luxurious avenue of elms.

On a hill which once overlooked the lake that
emptied into the city of Johnstown in 1889 is the
Max Moorehead "cottage."

The structural elements of a simple, upper story
wooden porch show the strong sense of design
among the early builders of the South Fork
Fishing and Hunting Club Cottages.

*A Victorian harmony of forms in a corner detail
of the Philander Knox Cottage.*

45

streams came cascading down the hillside. Cernik heard it running inside the walls of his Suzuki showroom. To relieve the pressure, his sons took hammers and chisels and made small holes in the walls at floor level every four feet. Then Cernik went out in his tow truck to push a friend's pickup out of water. When he returned, he heard one of his sons hollering that "the motorcycles are floating in water." Returning to the showroom, he unlocked the door, turned on the lights. The room was flooded. A few minutes later there was an explosion. Outside the showroom, Cernik saw Suzuki motorcycles flying out the windows.

He wasn't hurt, and to this day he is not sure what caused the explosion; he thinks it was in the showroom's gas heater. But the worst was yet to come on that warm summer evening in Johnstown.

Cernik returned to his home, which was not flooded. The All-Star baseball game played that night was over, so he sat on his porch and witnessed the rain, thunder and lightning. Then he heard a roar and saw tanks of propane rolling down the hill along Cooper Avenue. A dam owned by a local water company had broken in the hills; the water was rushing down the road, sweeping away homes and pushing cars and objects in front of it.

He recalls what he and his wife did next: "We had to get out of the house and up the hillside where it was safe. My wife grabbed the toaster and an electric pot—it's funny what you try to save in an emergency. I thought about my brand-new T-Bird. I jumped in the car, which was standing in several feet of water. I don't know how I got it started. The car just leaped forward in the water, and I turned up the hill onto safe ground."

The wave from the dam finally crashed into the Conemaugh, causing the already overflowing river to reverse direction and rush back toward Johnstown, wreaking havoc in the city. A total of 85 people were killed that night. "We lost our tow trucks, our gas station," Cernik says. "We could have had loss of life. We were just so hurt we didn't know what to do. My

A plaque on the base of the Grandview Cemetery memorial to the unidentified victims of the flood.

wife wanted to leave. But we had three sons who depended on our businesses for their livelihoods. So we thought we would try to get re-established, then we'd go."

It took the Cerniks a few days to clean up and get their businesses back in operation. Soon they were expanding again, with no thought of leaving. With the help of a Small Business Administration loan, he bought 58 prime acres in the area from a man who just happened to stop at his garage to make a phone call. On it he built a new motorcycle shop and an office for his businesses. The next year he bought an automatic car wash. And two years after that, hearing rumors of a coming nationwide shortage of nails, he acquired a nail mill from Bethlehem's Sparrows Point plant in Baltimore, shipping 42 tractor-trailer loads of nail equipment and machines back to his domains in Tanneryville.

A graying, powerful man in his 50s, who seems most comfortable in baseball cap, jeans and sportshirt, Ed Cernik believes strongly that "those who receive should give back," and he has given back in many ways. Cernik was one of the leaders in the reconstruction that followed the '77 flood. On the weekend he was interviewed, he was hard at work in his bulldozer, leveling some land on the hill overlooking his properties into a picnic ground for Johnstown residents.

*The river waters which flow through
the heart of Johnstown.*

BEGINNINGS

Water, coal, iron and steel, and railroads have shaped the history of Johnstown—and the character of its people. The story begins with water, which has been both a blessing and a curse.

The Little Conemaugh and Stonycreek rivers drain some 620 square miles of Appalachian tableland before twisting and cutting through their rocky channels into the valley. Innumerable mountain springs and creeks—Solomon's Run, Sam's Run, Laurel Run—trickle and race downhill into the rivers.

In the 19th century, abundant wildlife roamed the mountains—pheasants, wild geese, ruffed grouse, wild turkeys, even black bear and wildcats. One writer described "graceful slopes and frowning precipices robed in darkest green of hemlock and spruce. Open fields here and there verdant with young grass and springing grain, or moist and brown beneath the plow for planting time. Hedgerow and underwood fragrant with honeysuckle and wild blackberry bloom; violets and geraniums purpling the forest floor."

The Delaware Indians named the mountain stream that became a river in Johnstown "Gunamonki" or "Cough-naugh-maugh"—meaning "little otter" or "otter creek." According to Nathan Shappee, natives of the valley and travelers alike noted the Conemaugh's purity and clearness. "Salmon and trout swarmed in the river beds before the mine water was drained into

A grove of trees on the hillside adjacent
to the Inclined Plane, seen through an
early morning mist.

*An idyllic view from the former dam site of Lake
Conemaugh which burst during the 1889 flood
and filled the entire valley.*

*Portrait bust of the founder of
Johnstown, Joseph Schantz (Johns), on
the memorial in Central Park.*

ZUM GEDÄCHTNIS AN
JOSEPH SCHANTZ
GRÜNDER DER
STADT JOHNSTOWN
ERRICHTET ZUM
HUNDERTSTEN JAHRES-
TAGE SEINES TODES
18. JANUAR 1813
VON BÜRGERN DEUTSCHER
ABKUNFT VON JOHNSTOWN
ENTHÜLLT 15. JUNI, 1913

*Plaque on the pedestal of the
Central Park memorial.*

the channels," wrote Shappee in his 1940 thesis. "Men and boys would 'brush' the Stonycreek to drive fish into rock traps where they would be killed and then divided among the hunters. In autumn hunters would shoot wild ducks on the Stonycreek just south of the Poplar Street Bridge. Sometimes the migrating birds would fly against the big stack of the Cambria Iron Company where workmen would retrieve the stunned fowls."

The first white settlers did not arrive in the valley until the 1770s. Before that a few Indian paths crossed the mountains, but nothing that could be described as a road led into and out of the valley. A treaty with the Indians in 1768 opened up the territory to white settlers. The first to arrive were two brothers, Solomon and Samuel Adams, who established farms and built a road. Samuel and his sister, Rachel, were killed fleeing from Indians. The last Indian resident of the valley, Shappee reported, "bore the unromantic name of Joe Wipey and was killed by John Hinckston and James Cooper in May 1774."

Joseph Schantz, the town's founder, arrived in the valley in 1794 and built a log cabin near a spring that fed into the Stonycreek. Schantz, who became Joseph Johns—probably after the German name was ground down by the natives' pronunciation—cleared about 30 acres for farming. In 1800, he laid out a town, obtained a charter for it, and began selling lots.

Johns hoped that his settlement would become a trading center and a county seat. But the lots in the narrow valley were too small for farming and attracted only a few tradesmen and innkeepers who hoped to see a town spring up in the wilderness. When Ebensburg, 18 miles away, was declared the seat of a new county—called Cambria, the old Roman name for Wales—Johns did not hang around for long; after 13 years in the valley, he sold the town and moved to nearby Somerset County.

The westward movement of wagon trains largely bypassed this hidden valley. The few people who did settle in the area came to harvest timber in the hills. As late as 1803, there were only three families living in the town established by Johns, then called Conemaugh Old Town. The town began to come alive when owners of the first iron foundries in the Juniata and Shade Valleys realized it was a convenient point of entry to a water highway to the west. They sent their iron by road over the mountains to the town, where it was stored in depots until the rivers rose in the spring, then shipped down the Conemaugh on flatboats, or "arks."

The construction of a canal system across the state, from Philadelphia to Pittsburgh, opened up the town to the outside world for the first time. Peter Levergood, the second proprietor of Johnstown, offered the state land in Conemaugh Old Town for a canal basin at the head of the western branch.

Turning the rivers and mountain streams of western Pennsylvania into a well-regulated canal system was a monumental task. The western division, running from Pittsburgh to Johnstown, required 64 locks, 16 aqueducts, 64 culverts, and 152 bridges. About eight and a half acres on the

*Testing rails at the Cambria Iron
Company in the 1890s.*

banks of the Little Conemaugh were excavated for the crescent-shaped basin in downtown Johnstown. Upon its completion in 1830, Johnstown became a busy harbor town. Wharves and warehouses and repair shops and hotels lined the basin. The persistent horns of arriving canal boats became a familiar daily sound. News and gossip of the outside world were exchanged. Large numbers of strangers—traders, travelers, craftsmen and professional men, shippers, canal men—flowed in and out of the city for the first time in its history.

The only obstacle to linking the eastern and western branches of the canal system was the Allegheny Mountain between Hollidaysburg and Johnstown. To transport canal boats over the mountain, the state built a portage railroad with a series of 10 "inclined planes" to get up and down the steepest portions. A steam engine at each peak lifted cars up each incline on pulleys and then lowered them, with the weight of the ascending cars balancing that of the descending cars. The inclines were connected by stretches of level track on which the cars were pulled at first by horses and later by steam locomotives. To ease the transfer of cargo and passengers from the rail to the canal stretches, a canal boat was designed that could be taken apart in sections and later reassembled. The sections were loaded onto the cars at Hollidaysburg with passengers and freight inside. At the end of the 37-mile journey to Johnstown, they were put back together and placed in the canal basin through use of slips.

The Allegheny Portage Railroad, one of the engineering wonders of the age, was finished in 1834, the same year that the town of Conemaugh was officially renamed Johnstown. Among those who came through Johnstown on a canal journey was the novelist Charles Dickens, who was bored by his fellow passengers but thrilled by the dizzying ride on the portage railroad. "Occasionally the rails are laid upon the extreme verge of a giddy precipice," Dickens wrote in *American Notes,* "and looking from the carriage window, the traveller gazes sheer down, without a stone or

From 1830 to 1854, Johnstown was one of the major stops along the Pennsylvania Mainline Canal. This photo of a drawing by George Storm shows boats as they pass through a covered aqueduct over the Little Conemaugh River and into the Canal Basin there.

scrap of fence between, into the mountain depths below. The journey is very carefully made, however; only two carriages traveling together; and while proper precautions are taken, it is not to be dreaded for its dangers."

Dickens continued: "It was very pretty traveling thus, at a rapid pace along the heights of the mountain in a keen wind, to look down into a valley full of light and softness; catching glimpses through the tree-tops, of scattered cabins; children running to the doors; dogs bursting out to bark, whom we could see without hearing; terrified pigs scampering homewards; families sitting out in their rude gardens; cows gazing upward with a stupid indifference; men in their shirt-sleeves looking on at their unfinished houses, planning out tomorrow's work; and we riding onward, high above them, like a whirlwind. It was amusing, too, when we had dined and rattled down a steep pass, having no other moving power than the weight of the carriages themselves, to see the engine released, long after us, come buzzing down alone, like a great insect, its back of green and gold

Built just after the flood, the top of the Lenhart
building features elaborate decorative detail.

*Railroad tracks curving into Bethlehem
Steel's Gautier Division.*

so shining in the sun, that if it had spread a pair of wings and soared away, no one would have had occasion, as I fancied, for the least surprise. But it stopped short of us in a very business-like manner when we reached the canal: and, before we left the wharf, went panting up this hill again, with the passengers who had waited for our arrival for the means of traversing the road by which we had come."

The completion of the portage railroad brought other spectacles to Johnstown. Shappee reported: "In 1837, the townsmen turned out to see Chief Keokuk and his Sac and Fox tribesmen pass through the village. Gliding through the Conemaugh Gap at sunset, Keokuk, impressed by the beauty of the valley, led his braves in a prayer to the Great Spirit. The funeral cortege of President Harrison passed through Johnstown in 1841. When the remains of Zachary Taylor arrived at the depot, a solemn procession, headed by his faithful horse, Old Whitey, conducted the funeral party down Railroad Street to the boat slip."

In 1839, the town collected $149,000 in canal tolls and freight charges for the nine months' season. But though revenues from iron shipments increased in the 1840s, Johnstown's canal revenues began to shrink after 1851, according to Shappee, reaching a trifling $1,651.83 in 1854. That was the year that the Pennsylvania Railroad completed its track over the mountains. The railroad line now spanned the state. The canal system could not compete. After only 20 years in operation, the state system was sold to its rival, the Pennsylvania Railroad, and soon abandoned.

With the coming of the railroads, the city's growth did not miss a beat; in fact, the tempo was stepped up. Johnstown became a stop on the main line of the Pennsylvania Railroad and was connected with the Baltimore & Ohio. The railroads provided an impetus for large-scale development of the region's mineral wealth, which had been well explored in the 1840s.

A local merchant, George King, owner of four small iron furnaces in the area, foresaw a growing demand for rails and with a partner, a former

Juniata ironmaster named Peter Schoenberger, made plans to build a rail rolling mill. Tracing the course of an iron deposit he had discovered at nearby Laurel Run, King found that it led straight to Prospect Hill in Johnstown. There, the two partners built their mill on bottom land at the foot of the mountain.

Up to that time, the small backwoods iron forges in the Alleghenies had produced mostly agricultural tools and household items for local use. The King-Schoenberger venture, like all such budding enterprises at the time, required steady nerves and large injections of capital. It was in financial trouble from the start. When the company went bankrupt in 1856, the iron works was leased to a Philadelphia firm, Wood, Morrell & Company. Over the next few years, Wood, Morrell bought up Cambria Iron bonds, and, at the end of its lease in 1862, when the owners were unable to honor the bonds, took full control of the company.

Under the firm but paternal hand of one of the investors, Daniel Justin Morrell, who had come to Johnstown as general manager in 1856, the Cambria Iron Works not only stabilized but grew into what was known far and wide as a magnificent enterprise. His contemporaries praised Morrell, a Quaker who had been raised on a farm in Maine, as a model of the enlightened capitalist. To a popular biographer and lecturer of the time, James Parton, Morrell proved irrefutably that "a king of business is a king of men." Parton said that Morrell was "a judge of men who knows how to pick the men he wants and keeps them by treating them as he would like to be treated in their place."

Morrell displayed all of the contradictions of the capitalist giants of the era. Since the American worker was "subject to no fetters of class or caste," Morrell said, he deserved to live "in a house not a hut" and to "wear good clothes and eat wholesome and nourishing food." Accordingly, the company set up a welfare system that took care of the worker virtually from the cradle to the grave.

At the same time, Morrell kept wages low—during the 1850s unskilled men might earn $1 a day, boys 37½ cents—and even reduced them during slow times. Anyone who tried to form a union or organize a work stoppage was summarily fired. When strikes did occur, the company hired armed police to combat them. To trade unionists, Morrell's rule was a form of tyranny. The *Iron Molder's Journal,* describing Johnstown, said: "If there is a town in Europe to compare with it in the actual serfdom of its inhabitants, we have failed to hear of it."

One man who objected to Morrell's policy of keeping wages low was William R. Jones, a tough Welshman who was one of the most highly respected plant managers in the industry. Captain Bill Jones, as he was known, thought the morale of his workers was important and on occasion shut down his department to take them to baseball games and horse races. When the plant's chief engineer died, Jones did not get his expected promotion, and so left Cambria to join Andrew Carnegie's Edgar Thompson Works on the banks of the Monongahela River in Pittsburgh, taking with him considerable knowledge of the new Bessemer processes. Some 200 workers from Johnstown followed him to the Edgar Thompson Works.

Of course, Morrell was not alone in paying low wages and squelching any signs of unionism. America's steelmakers were forced to keep down costs in order to be competitive. A capable and friendly manager, Morrell presided over the growth of an industry—and a burgeoning city. During his 29-year reign, the company emerged as one of the nation's biggest steelmakers, and the population of the valley went from a few thousand to nearly 30,000. Morrell probably did not have more than two years of a grade-school education; he had worked in a dry-goods business in Philadelphia before coming to Johnstown. But he mastered the techniques of the ironmaking business quickly and began associating with industry pioneers such as William Kelly, Alexander Holley, John Fritz and his brother George Fritz. The first industrial laboratory was established at the Cambria Works

The Kelly converter and the three-high rolling mill, both invented at Johnstown in the late nineteenth century, represent technologies which revolutionized the American steel industry.

KELLY
STEEL CONVERTER
USED AT
CAMBRIA IRON WORKS
1861 - 1862
THE PIONEER CONVERTER OF AMERICA

in 1860. Johnstown became known as a place where the frontiers of the technology were pushed forward.

John Fritz came to the Cambria Works before Morrell, soon after the first rails had been rolled. Formerly superintendent of the iron works in Norristown, Pennsylvania, he had accepted the superintendent's job at Johnstown in 1853. He was appalled by what he found. The mill used low-quality iron from local blast furnaces. The rails often cracked and split in the rolling process. The mill was not turning out enough good rolls fast enough to be profitable.

To strengthen the raw iron and make it into rails, it had to be "rolled"—the mass-production equivalent of the blacksmith hammering it into shape. The first rolling mill at Johnstown consisted of two rolls, one above the other. A bar of raw iron—the "pile"—was reheated and passed between the rolls through grooves; each groove was a template that imparted one or another feature of the rail's shape. A worker on one side of the rails picked up the red-hot bar with tongs and fed it into a groove. The rolls, powered by a steam engine, kept the bar moving to the other side, where a second worker picked it up and passed it back over the top to the first. Then, the first worker fed the bar into a second groove and the process was repeated.

Fritz's three-high rolling mill was a small innovation that revolutionized railmaking. By adding a third roll, the bar could be passed through one groove and then, on the other side, sent back through a second. The process was continuous, and quicker; the metal would not begin to cool, which was the main cause of cracking. Fritz's three-high mill turned out more rails, with fewer losses, and propelled the Cambria Works to the front ranks of the nation's producers.

Another innovator who came to Johnstown was William Kelly, a kettlemaker from Eddyville, Kentucky. Kelly had discovered that when drafts of air were blown through molten iron, the melting mass glowed fiercely and produced a superior metal that was relatively free of carbon; the oxygen in the air was burning the carbon away, although Kelly probably did not understand the process. Morrell gave a corner of the yard at the Cambria Works to the man whom skeptical workers referred to as "the Irish crank," to continue experiments with his crude converter.

Kelly had discovered the basic principle of mass-producing high-quality steel cheaply. Whether he did so before William Bessemer in England is a matter of long-standing controversy. Although Morrell had encouraged Kelly's experiments, the Cambria Works did not build a Bessemer furnace until 1871, after five other iron works in the United States had done so. George Fritz, Cambria's chief engineer, designed the plant with the assistance of Alexander Holley, the principal proponent of Bessemer steelmaking. By that time, the demand for steel was soaring as railroads sought more durable rails to take the pounding of its heavier locomotives and rolling stock. In the 1870s the Cambria Works was producing more steel rails than any of the other dozen or so railmaking plants in the country.

Just 20 years after its founding, the Cambria Works was a huge enterprise sprawling over 60 acres in Johnstown and employing 7,000. It owned 40,000 acres of valuable mineral lands in a region with a ready supply of iron, coal and limestone. It had its own brick works, coke ovens, flour mill, woolen factory and railroad. On the Westmont hill, it maintained farms to grow feed for the horses and mules that did much of the hauling inside the mills. Each of the company's plants had its own police and fire departments.

Life in Johnstown in the 1880s was a lot of hard work for everybody, but, as David McCullough points out in his history, *The Johnstown Flood*, at least "people had the feeling they were getting somewhere. The country seemed hell-bent for a glorious new age, and Johnstown was right up there booming along with the best of them." And if progress meant workers sometimes put in 12-hour days, six-day weeks and, occasionally, back-to-back shifts of 24 hours, well, they could seek relief in one of 123 saloons in the city.

But Daniel Morrell said that he wanted to create "a civilized, intelligent, Christian community" in Johnstown and not live "in the midst of ignorant and turbulent savages." The company built a library for the town and endowed it with a fund to pay for books and salaries. It organized night classes for boys who worked in the mills in mathematics, metallurgy, mechanical drawing and other subjects. It gave generous support to a scientific institute formed by the library association that offered classes to older workers.

The relative isolation of the valley and distance from larger cities required Cambria to take care of most of its employees' needs. The company built inexpensive homes that it rented to workers at low rates or encouraged them to buy with commercial mortgages. Though some of the buildings thrown up to house the lowest skilled workers were described as shanties made out of rough pine board—probably worse than the "huts" deplored by Morrell—other company-built dwellings were good-quality, structures of two or three stories with porches and small backyards.

In the same benevolent spirit, the company introduced the amenities of city life such as street paving and a water system. It maintained a company store that sold meat from livestock raised on company farms, flour and cereal from the company flour mill, and cloth from the woolen factory. The store was stocked with "an amazing variety of merchandise," according to one account, and employed 500 people. During recessions, when workers were laid off, they could often buy on credit in the store. The company also maintained an abbatoir in Johnstown where some 20 head of cattle and 75 to 100 sheep, hogs and calves were slaughtered each week. In addition, workers received medical care in a company-built hospital—the first industrial hospital in America.

Cambria employees were thus almost wholly dependent upon the company for life's requirements. So long as they did not band together to demand higher wages, they benefited from one of the most far-reaching and well-organized welfare systems ever devised. As John William Bennett wrote in a Ph.D. thesis entitled "Iron Workers in Woods Run and Johnstown: The Union Era, 1865–1885":

"The system [at] Cambria was made so thorough that a workingman in the employ of the corporation had no excuse for demanding payment of wages as such. The pass-book and store-order constituted the only currency with which its employees were familiar. Not only did the company supply them with all the necessities and luxuries they required 'at our current prices,' but it also provided them with tailors and shoemakers. In case of illness, a company physician was called in, and his fees paid in orders on the store. When there was a wedding or christening, the company clergyman performed the ceremony."

Daniel Morrell reigned supreme, a benign but total ruler who was also president of the Johnstown water works and gas works and sat on the boards of all the banks in town. He even got himself elected to Congress, where he advocated legislation to protect the growing American industry from cheaper rails produced in Britain. With two groups of partners, Morrell acquired the patents for the Kelly-Bessemer process and formed the Pneumatic Process Association, which sold licenses for Bessemer steelmaking. The steelmakers then set up a consortium for maintaining rail prices by allocating production quotas for the members (much like the OPEC oil countries today).

Morrell died in 1885, before the Great Flood. By the end of the century, Cambria had passed its peak. The demand for rails had slackened. Iron ore discovered in northern Michigan, the Lake Superior region, and the Mesabi Range in Minnesota yielded a higher-quality metal than local sources around Johnstown. The cost of transporting ore from distant fields made it difficult for Cambria to compete in making raw steel with producers closer to these sources. As the demand for steel grew in the Far West, moreover, plants on the Great Lakes and the Ohio River were better positioned to ship it more cheaply by water to the new markets.

Cambria thus lost its ability to compete in basic steelmaking and was forced to concentrate on making specialty-steel products. The industry's center of gravity shifted to Pittsburgh, where Carnegie's empire was growing by cutting costs, plowing profits back into the business and swallowing up competitors. Carnegie's foresight in moving into the manufacture of structural steel for bridges and buildings also helped his company forge into the industry lead.

Ultimately, his U.S. Steel controlled more resources than the Cambria Works ever did. Cambria, recapitalized in 1898 as the Cambria Steel Company, continued to grow as a major producer of specialty steel products such as car wheels, axles and steel plates. But the company had lost its momentum in developing new technology. On the eve of World War I, the

company was bought by a munitions maker, the Midvale Steel and Ordnance Company, which sold it to Bethlehem Steel in 1923. During two world wars and the postwar boom of the late 1940s and '50s, output was robust in Johnstown. Employment reached a peak of 18,000 in the 1950s. But it sank to about 2,500 as a result of a radical restructuring of Bethlehem's production in recent years. A leaner operation, under a far different management, is now emerging in Johnstown, as we shall see—one that may well recapture some of the spirit of its illustrious forbear.

"Cambria became a symbol in the history of the iron and steel industry," wrote Jeanne McHugh of the American Iron and Steel Association in *Alexander Holley and the Makers of Steel*. "For a generation or more, it was the training ground for the countless young men who entered the iron industry in America. The pattern for that training had been established by George Fritz's brother John, first at Cambria and later at the Bethlehem Iron Company, and for years a man could present no finer reference than to say that he had been one of Uncle John Fritz's boys."

Volunteer Fighting Associations were popular pastimes in early Johnstown. Founded in 1853, the Vigilant Volunteers Fire Company became a social group when it was replaced in 1906 by professional firefighters.

Rooted in old world traditions, this Carpatho-Russian wedding party was photographed at St. Mary's Byzantine Church, Cambria City.

ETHNIC ROOTS

Tossed together in a bowl in the mountains, a close, smoky cauldron, the diverse nationality and racial groups that came to Johnstown did not melt so easily but clung to their separate identities for dear life.

Prejudices ran deep. The values of custom and tradition were the only lifeboats in the struggle to survive. They not only made life bearable but gave it meaning. Although this ethnic heritage has gradually faded with every passing generation, it has left a lasting mark.

Jerry Davitch, 47 years old, grew up in Benscreek, one of the small towns bordering on Johnstown, in a neighborhood with about 25 homes built by Bethlehem Steel. "Fifteen of those homes had ethnic families in them," says Davitch, who is now Johnstown's deputy superintendent of schools. "You could have closed your eyes and you'd be in Yugoslavia.

"There was an incredible bond between these people. There was great love for older people. There was absolutely complete love for babies, for children. In my neighborhood you were raised by everybody; anybody could hold you, and anybody could discipline you. And if they disciplined you, you never went home and told your mother. There was a lot more love than discipline."

All four of Davitch's grandparents came from Yugoslavia at the turn of the century. "They were super, super people who walked across Europe to get a boat," he says. "When they got here, they worked from dawn till dark. I think often of the sacrifices they made. Sometimes, on days when I am not working as hard as I should, I feel I am cheating them. In the minds of the new generation, there is no such thing as sacrifice. Some of them won't walk to the corner store for a container of milk."

Life in Johnstown was a bubbling goulash with subtle seasoning. Though Davitch's grandparents were all from Yugoslavia, his father's family were Serbs and his mother's, Croatians—highly nationalistic groups that had trouble coexisting in the old country. The two groups spoke a similar Slavic language, but the Serbs wrote in Cyrillic and worshipped in the Eastern Orthodox Church while the Croatians used the Roman alphabet and were Roman Catholics. Davitch's father's family wanted to give him a Serbian name, but his mother held out for Jerry. He was baptized in the Eastern Orthodox Church, but when his coal-miner father died—"of all those good things you get when you work all your life in a coal mine"— Jerry was baptized again in the Roman Catholic Church of his mother.

The first group into Johnstown's ethnic pot were South Germans with names such as Fronheiser, Swegler, Kosta and Studeny, who joined the native Americans in the valley in the 1830s, during the canal era. They were followed in the next 20 years by Hessians with names such as Hubner, Baumer, Wehn, Young and Ludwig. Many of the Germans became merchants, but later arrivals worked in the mills; hundreds came under contract through agencies in New York that recruited labor for the Cambria Works. By 1880, German and Swedish contract labor was coming to Johnstown by the carload. (Contract labor was outlawed in Cambria County in 1885.)

English-speaking immigrants were drawn to the valley by railroad building, discoveries of coal and iron and the burgeoning Cambria Works. The first Irish came to help build the canal system and the portage railroad. Welsh people, Scottish and Cornish men (nicknamed "Cousin Jacks") came to work in coal mining and iron making. Many of these coal miners from

*New immigrants attending
Americanization classes at the
Johnstown YMCA after the
first World War.*

Britain were independent craftsman who worked on a contract system, owned their own powder for blasting and tools for cutting, and hired younger men to work with them. They brought traditions of democracy and experience with British unions that made them more willing to organize than millhands.

The influx from East Central Europe began about 1870 and further confused the ethnic stew. These agrarian peoples had lived for centuries under feudal monarchies that were constantly at war over borders and fighting off invaders. They were Slavic peoples—Serbs and Croats; Slovenes from what is now Yugoslavia; Poles, whose country had been repeatedly partitioned, and Slovaks who were long under the domination of Austro-Hungary. There were also Magyars (Hungarians), who spoke a language with an Urgo-Finnish root; Ukrainians from north of the Carpathian Mountains and Ruthenians from south of the Carpathians. When the Cambria Works began booming, the trickle of people from Eastern and Southern Europe grew into a flood as the demand for unskilled labor in the mills rose and the company did everything it could to encourage immigration. The tide reached its peak in the pre-World War I years.

Ewa Morawska, a scholar at the University of Pennsylvania, has described the upheavals that brought these peasant peoples to America in her

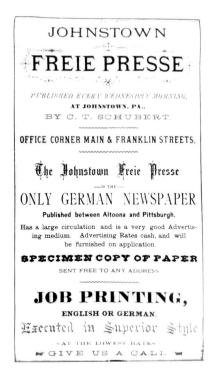

A German language newspaper, The Johnstown Freie-Presse, *was published in the late nineteenth century and continued until the beginning of World War I.*

book, *For Bread With Butter: The Life-Worlds of East Central Europeans in Johnstown, Pennsylvania, 1890–1940.* Morawska shows that after the breakup of the feudal system in Eastern Europe land became concentrated in the hands of a few wealthier farmers and the holdings of the poorer peasants became smaller and smaller as they were divided among their heirs. Unable to make a living on the land, millions of peasants began criss-crossing Europe looking for seasonal work in cities.

Many of the more adventurous came to America, stimulated by the letters that came back from the first to cross the ocean. Their aspirations were modest when they arrived: to earn enough to send money and gifts back home; to save enough to return to their villages and buy a few more hectares or a cow, or build a larger house; to give their families a margin of security above mere subsistence.

Upon their arrival, these rural peoples were shocked by the smoke and grime and noise of an industrial city. At first they were housed in company-built tenements, called "Rotten Row," which appear to have been located in Cambria City across the river from the Lower Works, but which were evidently torn down and rebuilt at least twice. Slowly, the various groups gravitated to areas that resembled the topographical features of their homelands. As Morawska described this gradual movement:

"The Slovaks from the highest mountain regions of Spiš tended to settle up on the hills, in the boroughs of Lower Yoder and Brownstown; the Magyars, on the other hand, chose to live in the 'lowland' region of Cambria City. The Poles from the hilly Limanowa Region in Galicia, as well as the Ukrainians from Lesko and the [Ruthenians] from the other side of the Carpathians, settled either in the hilly parts of Minersville or on the slopes in East Conemaugh. The 'lowland' Congress Poles, however, like the Magyars, preferred flat land in Cambria City."

Getting even an unskilled job in the mills meant having a relative or a member of one's ethnic group in charge of a work gang. The gangs were organized along ethnic lines, many of which were made up of fathers and sons. As long as the demand for rails held steady, there was work. But periodic recessions led to layoffs and threatened the precarious budgets of immigrant families. Their fortunes rose and sank and then rose again. Many left to seek work elsewhere; the immigrants had a high transiency rate, Morawska's studies show. Many families took in boarders to help meet expenses; wives cleaned house and cooked for their large families and often as many as 10 boarders. Virtually everybody who could kept a garden and raised chickens and other livestock to help feed the household.

"The wish to survive, not to 'go under,' was solidly embedded in the minds of the immigrants," Morawska writes. In the highly stratified societies from which they had come, they had occupied the lowest rung on the ladder. They had been taught the virtues of patience, humility, and thrift. Work was valued for its own sake, not just for what it earned.

In Johnstown, the majority tended to lump them all together as "Hungarians," or "Hunkies," and sought to educate them to American ways during the periodic "Americanization" campaigns that were common in this era. They, in turn, looked upon "the Americans" as an alien culture into which they had little chance of acceptance.

So they retreated into what Morawska describes as their own "life-worlds." They organized their own churches, founded branches of their national societies and lodges, published their own native-language newspapers, formed their own competing sport clubs and leagues. Their lives were woven tightly into a rich tapestry of weddings, balls, picnics, national celebrations, elections of lodge officers—all within the confines of their own group and closely related groups.

While maintaining their separate ways, however, the various groups started to discover things they had in common. This early cooperation was the first glimmering of a larger sense of community. German-speaking Slovaks were able to mingle with older residents of German background and even get jobs through them in the mills. Serbs and Croats found common cause, according to Morawska, through the efforts of a "dynamic Serb" in Johnstown who was admired by both groups and served as president of both the Serbian and Croatian societies.

Older and larger ethnic groups welcomed newcomers of other nationalities into their churches. For example, in the 1880s, Morawska found, Slavs and Magyars residing in the "Rotten Row" tenements of Cambria City attended St. Mary's Immaculate Conception German Catholic Church. During the first decade of this century, St. Mary's Greek Catholic Church served Slovaks and Ruthenians as well as Magyar-speaking immigrants from Gemer, Ung, and Spiš counties in Hungary, with one Mass in Slavish and one in Hungarian every Sunday.

When their numbers and resources grew, each group tended to seek its own pastor and build its own church. As parishioners moved out to the

The YWCA building was once one of Johnstown's grand mansions.

surrounding hills, they built more churches. In Johnstown, when floods destroyed one church a grander one soon went up in its place.

St. John Gualbert, the Roman Catholic church built largely for Irish parishioners in the 1830s, was in the path of destruction of '89 but survived, only to burn when a house that had washed against it caught fire and ignited the church. A new church built in 1895 on Clinton Street was damaged, but not so extensively, in the 1936 and 1977 floods. St. John Gualbert, which now has the status of a cathedral of the Johnstown-Altoona diocese, has been constantly refurbished and embellished. With its two bell towers—the taller one a replica of the Campanile in Venice—it remains one of the most impressive of the city's churches. The bronze doors, made in Italy as part of a 1971 remodeling, portray scenes from the life of St. John Gualbert, a 12th-century Florentine from a noble family whose path to canonization began when he sheathed his sword and did not take revenge on his brother's murderer.

Amid Greater Johnstown's numerous churches are many small treasures. In Cambria City, St. Mary's Greek Catholic Church has at least 10 different patterns of brickwork in its facade; inside, over the altar, is a beautiful mosaic baldacchino imported from Pecs, Hungary. On the same street is St. Casimir's, an imposing Romanesque-style building with a large rose window and a statue of St. Casimir at its base. The Cambria Steel Company donated the steel and bricks for the church, built for the Polish congregation in 1920. By arrangement with the priest, the company regularly deducted money from the paychecks of Polish workers for the church's upkeep.

Smaller minorities also gathered in Johnstown. The first Jewish clothing merchants came during the hectic decade of the 1850s, mainly from the Hesse-Darmstadt region of Germany. Other Jews followed on the heels of immigrants from the villages of Eastern Europe. Over the years Jewish families and their descendants established some of the biggest and

The beautiful gothic interior of the
Immaculate Conception Church.

Looking up at the facade
of the Immaculate Conception Church.

The archangel Michael on the exterior
of St. Stephen's Church.

These casts of a pulpit by Luca della Robbia in Florence, Italy, are now in the Flood Museum collection. They were saved from the facade of the Joseph Johns Junior High School.

This remarkable gargoyle on the facade of the
Immaculate Conception Church is an example of
the fine gothic stonework found in a number of
Johnstown's churches.

best-known dry goods and department stores in the city, among them Nathan's, Schwartz's, Kline's and Glosser Brothers.

Blacks came from Cumberland, Maryland, before 1840, to work in William Rosensteel's tannery stripping hides from animals in baths of malodorous chemicals. More blacks came to the city during the general migration north in the second decade of this century. During a steel strike in 1919, the company recruited blacks as well as Mexicans to replace striking workers in the mills. In these early years, black workers were regarded with suspicion and segregated; they even had separate lavoratories.

For all their incredible diversity, the suspicions, the fears, the taunts, there seem to have been few violent confrontations among Johnstown's ethnic communities. Perhaps because each group retreated into its own cultural shell to minimize friction, or because the all-powerful company would not have tolerated conflict, or because power was fractured among so many groups, they learned to get along and to live at peace.

Learning to assert their rights against the company took longer. Because in the beginning they believed their sojourn in the United States was to be short, they would not risk joining unions. The ethnic organization of work gangs in the mills further inhibited unionism; it was a deliberate strategy to prevent working-class solidarity from developing, in Morawska's view. Even when they did join picket lines, they stood with members of their own group. Not until the 1920s did ethnic-group members turn to unions in large numbers to demand an end to such conditions as 12-hour days and six-day weeks. Because of broad popular pressure, the steel industry did away with the 12-hour day in 1921. By then, they knew they were in America to stay. Many had fought for the country in a world war; they were ready to stand up for their rights as Americans.

With so many minority groups living together, Johnstowners had learned important lessons in tolerance. They learned not only to respect differences, but to appreciate them. To Frances Hesselbein of the Girl

*Glosser Brothers' department store has been in
downtown Johnstown since the 1890s.*

A German-Hungarian sausage market, Krauss and Boharshik, photographed in the early 1900s, typifies Johnstown's ethnic mix.

Scouts, Johnstown was "a generous provider, and never greater than in its 'gift of example,' in the pluralism of its people."

Given an achievement award by the city several years ago, Hesselbein, who now resides in New York City, said in a speech: "I have never had to adjust to living in New York; I am very comfortable with the ethnic and racial mix in New York because I grew up in a town that welcomed people from all parts of Europe and their customs. Their cultures were shared abundantly. Some of the best food in the world has to be found at Johnstown wedding receptions—holupki, kolatchka, lasagna, chopped chicken livers—all bringing the wider world to the table."

Much of the charm of this concentrated mingling of cultures remains. This is a place where blacks can be overheard speaking Polish learned from friends and fellow workers. It is the apparent setting of a popular series of mystery novels by the pseudonymous K. C. Constantine, whose police chief hero, Mario Balzic, is of mixed ethnic parentage and can swear in

The Christ the Savior Carpatho-Russian Dance Troupe *performing at an ethnic festival in the Johnstown campus of the University of Pittsburgh.*

both Serbian and Italian. The fraternal organizations, the ethnic festivals, the choral societies, the children in peasant blouses dancing the polka, the Easter baskets covered with finely embroidered cloths, the church suppers of kolbassi, holupki, and kaputsa still give color and sweetness to life in Johnstown. Many Johnstowners who have long since moved to suburban towns return to their old neighborhoods for Sunday services and church activities.

Except for a few dynamic congregations, however, church membership has been declining. The old ties to neighborhood and tradition no longer have the same hold on the generations born after World War II. Anna Olchesky, a 72-year-old great-grandmother of Slovak descent who has lived in Cambria City almost all her life, recalls the old days and the mix of people in her neighborhood: "They all got along because they learned to," she says. "Everybody was neighborly; they helped you get the kids off to school, they helped with the washing. Today, most of the people

*St. John Gualbert is one of the city's most
impressive churches. The taller of the two bell
towers is modeled after the Venice Campanile.*

*A lovely mosaic of the Virgin Mary above the
doorway to St. Mary's Byzantine Catholic
Church in Cambria City.*

*Detail of a stained glass window created by
highly skilled artists for the Immaculate
Conception Church.*

*The Masonic Temple is an outstanding example
of art deco architecture with fine decorative
elements on the facade.*

"The Blessing of the Baskets" is an Easter custom still practiced by Catholics of East Central European heritage.

are second and third generation. They all seem to keep to themselves. They look at you, and if you're a little older, they don't have much to do with you."

The upheavals of a society on the move, of a high-tech, competitive economy, have inevitably seeped into this valley and eroded traditional neighborhood, family and community ties. But Johnstowners have held them off longer than most. The surprising thing is that people who grew up here and left have found their way back, as if seeking something lost along the way, even young people.

Pete Duranko was a pro football player, a defensive tackle for the Denver Broncos, for nine years. After retiring from football in 1975, Duranko, a graduate of Bishop McCort High School in Johnstown, left Denver to return to the area with his family. He went back to school to get a master's in industrial relations at St. Francis College in Loretto and is now personnel manager of the Abex Corporation. Duranko says that he and his

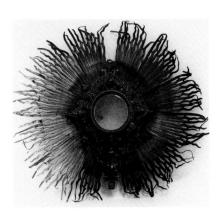

Left: *A "memory bottle" from the Johnstown Flood Museum, contains a variety of small objects found in the wreckage of the 1889 flood.* Right: *The surviving section of a monstrance from the Church of St. John Gualbert.*

wife chose to return because they wanted their two sons to grow up in secure surroundings, and they have family members still living in the community. "It's a friendly town," he says. "The people are concerned, hard-working and have a lot of pride. I liked the idea of my kids growing up in my hometown."

Diane Buck, whose grandparents were Slovak and Hungarian, left town for 10 years after graduating from high school. After earning a degree in special education from Indiana University of Pennsylvania, she taught in a small town in the Moshannon Valley and then at a school in Harrisburg, before returning three years ago to marry Paul Buck, whose family owns a hobby shop in Johnstown. Diane, who teaches children with social and emotional problems at Johnstown High School, was the first woman elected president of the Junior Chamber of Commerce. Like many other

Father George Johnson blessing the Little
Conemaugh River on the Russian Orthodox
New Year's Day.

returnees to Johnstown, she feels that the community offers a happy balance between a small-town atmosphere and the cultural advantages of a medium-sized city.

Jerry Davitch was an administrator of a very large school district with 5,000 teachers in Tucson, Arizona. When he decided to return to Johnstown in 1985, he had to take a 25 percent pay cut to become deputy superintendent, and he was returning to a district that had all the problems associated with declining enrollments. While shiny new schools were going up in neighboring towns, Johnstown itself had become an inner-city school district on a small scale with many aging schools built in the 1920s.

Davitch, who also coaches the high school football team, felt he could have a bigger impact in Johnstown's schools than in a district the size of Tucson. But he and his wife had two other strong reasons for wanting to resettle in Johnstown. "We had two very young children, four and six," he says. "Johnstown is one of the safest cities in the country to raise young children. In Tucson, we would never have let the children ride their bikes by themselves in the city—the risk of harm is small but we did not want to take it. In Johnstown, we feel very comfortable letting them go off on their own."

The pull of home was hard to resist. "I never left the place without a feeling of sadness," says Davitch, who has worked in several school districts around the country. "I always felt great about coming home. All of my immediate family are here now—my mother and brother. My brother was away for 12 years and every day thought about moving back.

"I have probably been in over 80 percent of this country," Davitch adds. "I have seen communities large and small. I feel fortunate that I spent my first 18 years in Johnstown. I will feel fortunate if I can spend my last 18 years in Johnstown. In the end, that's the best thing I can say about the place."

*Delicate ironwork and arches
grace the gothic interior of the
Immaculate Conception Church.*

*The memorial in Grandview Cemetery
commemorating 777 unidentified and unclaimed
dead from the flood of 1889.*

HELL AND
HIGH WATER

From the Gilgamesh Epic of the ancient Babylonians to Greek mythology and the Old Testament, to the legends of Chingpaw tribesmen in Burma and Papagos Indians in Arizona, the story of a great flood that threatens to end all human life on earth is nearly universal in the world's cultures.

Scholars are not sure why this should be so. Some say it is because all races and tribes through the ages have known disastrous floods. Others trace these stories back to a collective memory of the Creation, during which God commanded that "the waters under the heaven be gathered together unto one place." Rachel Carson in *The Sea Around Us* wrote about the formation of the oceans after the earth had cooled some 2.5 billion years ago: "Never have there been such rains since that time. They fell continuously, day and night, days passing into months, into years, into centuries."

If communities can have a collective memory, Johnstown's is deeply etched with stories of floods passed on by the generations, by the accounts of parents and grandparents, marvelous in the retelling, of fear and flight, of terrible grief mixed with moments of exalted bravery, of the communion with helping strangers and the triumph of building anew.

Floods were almost a yearly event in the valley during the 1880s. The

A drawing shows the wreckage of houses which
caught fire and burned through the night at the
stone bridge like a huge funeral pyre.

The broken dam of Lake Conemaugh which caused the disastrous flood.

rivers always ran high in the spring, sometimes filling the lower half of the town to the top step of buildings. Slag dumped into the rivers from the mills and encroachments on the river for construction narrowed the channels and seemed to worsen the flooding. People complained that the heavy pilings sunk in the Conemaugh for the stone railroad bridge in 1887 would raise water levels even more.

On the afternoon of May 30, 1889, following a quiet Memorial Day ceremony and a parade, it began raining in the valley. The rains became heavy during the night, and the next day water filled the streets of the town. There were rumors that a dam holding an artificial lake in the mountains to the northeast might give way. But those reports had been heard many times in the past, and they were ignored.

The dam had been built by the state between 1840 and 1852 to hold a reservoir that was to supply water for the canal basin at Johnstown during the dry months. When the canal was abandoned, the dam was sold. The owners in 1889 were a group of wealthy Pittsburgh businessmen, who had built up the dam to hold an artificial lake about two miles long and up to a mile wide for weekend and holiday recreation. The membership of the South Fork Hunting and Fishing Club included some of the most powerful figures of the era—Frick, Mellon, Carnegie, Philander Knox (later a U.S. senator, Attorney General and Secretary of State). The club left a caretaker in charge of the dam and paid little attention to structural defects that were apparent before the Great Flood. To keep fish in the lake, they placed wire-mesh screens over the spillway.

When the rain-swollen lake reached the top of the earthen dam on the afternoon of May 31, water started brimming over the sagging center of the breast—its weakest spot. Efforts to shore it up, to remove the debris-clogged screens and to dig a second spillway to relieve the pressure on the breast were too little and too late. The dam gave way at about 3:10 P.M. and an estimated 20 million tons of water began spilling into the winding gorge that led to Johnstown some 14 miles away.

The water had not yet reached full speed when it rushed past the town of South Fork, situated on a hillside. Below South Fork, it halted momentarily behind a stone viaduct, then, breaking through, fell with cataract force on the little village of Mineral Point, which was also in its path.

The wind stirred up by the powerful torrent blew houses right off their foundations. The lake followed the course of the Little Conemaugh, in effect, sliding down on top of an already overflowing river, sweeping away buildings, trees and bushes, railroad track and freight cars, and the corpses of animals and people. When it neared the railroad yards at East Conemaugh, an engineer, who had heard it, tied down the whistle on his locomotive, drove a short distance to the west and fled. The persistent whistle was a vague warning to residents of East Conemaugh. But Johnstown, still several miles away, received no clear signal of onrushing danger.

Militia men fend off potential looters on the
streets of Johnstown after the flood.

Harrisburg Telegram.

VOL. VII.   HARRISBURG, PA., SUNDAY, JUNE 9, 1889.   NO. 25

DEATH'S DREADFUL SWIRL!

The Most Appalling Calamity in American History Overtakes the Towns Along the Conemaugh River, Sweeping Away Hundreds of Homes and Multitudes of Human Beings.

9,000-PERSONS PERISH-9,000

An Artificial Lake Empties 'a Resistless Deluge Upon South Fork, Mineral Point, East Conemaugh, Johnstown, Cambria and Coopersdale, Causing an Unparalleled Loss of Life and Property.

FLOOD AND FLAME COMBINE THEIR TERRORS.

A RACE FOR HIS LIFE.

The Brave Engineer of Locomotive 1165 Crosses the Bridge at South Fork an Instant Before the Structure is Washed Away.

Headlines about the Johnstown flood in The Harrisburg Telegram.

By some accounts, when the grisly tide reached Johnstown at 4:07 P.M. it looked less like a wave than a huge, furiously tumbling ball of water and debris preceded by a cloud of dust. Hearing the screams and shouts from the streets, people scrambled to their attics and roofs or ran for the hillsides. There they watched helplessly as their friends and neighbors floated by on rooftops or clinging to trees. The mass of water and debris raced through the town like a giant on a drunken rampage. After the wave was split in two by the Franklin Street Methodist Church, the main part rushed toward the Stonycreek, bounded off the small mountain that is now Westmont hill and fell back into the Conemaugh River. Then came the most horrifying scenes of all. The mass of debris, live with human beings struggling to stay afloat, piled up at the stone railroad bridge and caught fire, probably as a result of leaking fuel from railroad cars or stoves—a ghastly funeral pyre.

Only a few known survivors of the Great Flood were alive in Johnstown in 1989, among them Elsie Frum, 106 years old, and Frank Shamo, 100 years old. Many moving eyewitness accounts have been left that attest to the enormity of the event. One letter to the Centennial

The enormous task of cleaning up the streets of Johnstown after the flood.

Committee, from a woman in Ohio, enclosed a detailed description of the flood left by her great-uncle, Warren B. Thomas. Thomas was one of five children of John Thomas, who owned a large dry-goods store in Johnstown. A little after 4 P.M. he had looked out his door and seen what looked like "a great cloud of powdered mortar." He yelled to his half brother, Isaac, "The reservoir is coming." The two men grabbed Isaac's wife and two children and started for the nearest hill. They never would have made it if two men had not come along on horses and helped them through the flood waters.

Through the rain, on top of what was then called Green Hill, Thomas saw the remaining moments of the flood drama. "Drenched to the skin, stunned, stupefied, wretched," he wrote, "I stand there in the darkness wondering about the fate of my family. Have they been lost in the flood? If not, will they be burned to death in that big fire raging down there?

"As I stood in the rain and looked over the whole panorama spread before me," Thomas continued, "what power on earth could ever describe the terrifying scene—the most appalling sight any human being could ever expect to see—a whole city being destroyed and thousands swept into eternity right before your eyes!"

The destruction in Johnstown had occurred in only about 10 minutes. What had been a thriving steel town with rows of two- and three-story

Survivors of the flood lining up to receive badly needed food and supplies.

frame homes for workers, with churches, saloons, a library, a railroad station with bright-colored awnings, electric street lights, a roller-skating rink, two opera houses, was buried under mud and debris.

The aftermath of the flood is one of the most intriguing chapters in American social history. The disaster coincided with a revolution in communications that was making one nation out of diverse regions and hundreds of isolated rural communities strung out across a continent. The railroads stretched from coast to coast. The telegraph was now a fixture, with thousands of miles of lines laid across country. Newspapers were growing in numbers and circulation; reporting was aggressive and the competition for readers' attention increasingly feisty.

For days papers across the country played up the details of the flood on their front pages in prose that was both gushingly sentimental and lurid. With rail lines into the city washed out, the first reporters to arrive came on foot over the mountains. Their dispatches filled the telegraph wires and

A bronze relief commemorating the flood mounted high up on the facade of the Wehn Building on Clinton Street.

brought relief teams of medical specialists and charity workers, along with souvenir hunters, drifters, and ladies of the American Christian Temperance Movement. Trainloads of food and supplies soon came from Pittsburgh and the far reaches of America; one train arrived with three cars full of coffins and 55 undertakers. Rumors spread of tramps and thieves picking among the bodies to find jewelry and other loot, while self-appointed policemen circulated through the city looking for culprits.

The help that came from beyond the hills was heartwarming to Johnstowners, who repaid it in later years with their generosity to other communities in similar straits. The 1889 flood witnessed the first truly national relief effort to aid disaster survivors. A total of nearly $4 million was collected for the Johnstown Relief Fund, from every state in the union and 14 foreign nations. At the age of 67, Clara Barton came to the city to distribute supplies and stayed for five months to assist in the rehabilitation of the town, earning the title of "the heroine of Johnstown." Although she and a team of 50 doctors sent by the Philadelphia Red Cross branch had strong disagreements, the flood established Barton's American Red Cross as the pre-eminent emergency relief organization in the U.S. An estimated 25,000 Johnstown residents received some form of direct aid from the Red Cross.

"No other calamity so involved the sentimental core of Victorian America," Nathan Shappee wrote. "The sudden rush of the Flood, the invasion of happy homes, the drowning of members of families, the pathetic recoveries of the dead—all made the Great Flood the monster of the mass mind. The Flood destroyed life when it was still very closely connected to the rural and village roots that supported American ideals and sentiments. The rewards of honest labor, the sanctity of the home, gallantry toward women, and an unwavering trust in the Almighty were all cut across by the path of the Conemaugh in 1889. The American people stopped aghast at the wholesale destruction of Johnstown; then threw all of

*A view of Clinton Street
with the Gautier division on the left.*

The Stonycreek River running under the
Franklin Street Bridge, with the First United
Methodist Church, a landmark of downtown
Johnstown, seen in the background.

The first United Methodist Church as framed by the steel girders of the Franklin Street Bridge.

A polished bronze relief on the pedestal
of the Joseph Schantz (Johns)
monument in Central Park.

their good sentiments into aiding the stricken survivors. In this mass charity stood revealed the patterns of emotionality in all their aspects. The good and the noble, the cheap and the tawdry, the unselfish, the mercenary, the honest and the truthful, the false and exaggerated—all played their part in making the Great Flood the symbol it has remained."

In a famous study of a more recent flood, at Buffalo Creek in West Virginia, the sociologist Kai T. Erickson concluded that the February 1972 disaster had destroyed not just the homes in the tiny coal-mining town but the spirit of the community. A grim 93 percent of 615 victims examined by psychiatrists a year and a half after the flood were found to be suffering from an identifiable emotional disorder. "Most of the survivors responded to the disaster with a deep sense of loss," Erickson wrote, "a nameless feeling that something had gone awry in the order of things, that their minds had been bruised beyond repair, that they would never again be able to find coherence, that the world as they knew it had come to an end."

Unlike Buffalo Creek, Johnstown began the work of reconstruction almost immediately, under 15 committees of the citizenry. Arthur Moxham, the local manufacturer who was set up as "dictator" to lead the effort, recognized that putting the townspeople to work cleaning up would help restore confidence and heal the spirit. Moxham opposed asking for troops from the National Guard, was irritated when the state quartermaster arrived with 200 workers from Pittsburgh, and resigned when other local leaders insisted that the residents could not do the job without outside help.

One of the initial sparks for recovery came from John Fulton, general manager of the Cambria Works. At the first church service following the disaster, Fulton stood up and announced that the flooded Cambria mills would be rebuilt. "Amen!" responded several voices. "Johnstown is going to be rebuilt," Fulton said. "Thank God!" came a voice.

"Get to work, clean up your department, set your lathes going again," Fulton continued. "The furnaces are all right, the steel works are all right.

Get to work, I say. Johnstown has had its day of woe and ruin. It will have its day of renewed prosperity. Labor, energy, and capital, by God's grace, shall make the city more thriving than ever in the past."

"Amen!" shouted the crowd.

The mills were back in operation within a month. As we have seen, the Cambria Works grew, and Johnstown became more prosperous than ever, just as Fulton had predicted it would. The disaster had not destroyed the community but strengthened it. The euphoria, good fellowship and altruism of the rebuilding process would carry over into the future. Later generations would draw on lessons learned in 1889.

When the second major disaster struck, on March 17, 1936, Greater Johnstown had a population of about 70,000. There had been an inordinate amount of snow that winter. On St. Patrick's Day afternoon, temperatures were warmer than normal and that, combined with intense rain, led to rapid melting of the thick snow cover in the hills. Once again water from the creeks and streams was rushing downhill into the rivers. By nightfall, the cold, murky water was spilling into the streets. A third of the town was submerged in waters up to 17 feet high, battering homes and businesses and stranding thousands on upper floors and rooftops.

Once again, the *déjà vu* scenes flickered across the community's collective screen. Tanks, poles, radios, tires, washing machines, refrigerators and wreckage of all sorts darted in and out of alleyways and bobbed through the streets, according to one account. Houses were swept off their foundations, automobiles crushed against buildings. Bridges cracked and crumbled under the pounding of the waters.

The next day, Johnstowners surveyed the wreckage. The damage to property, later estimated at almost $41 million, was larger than the destruction in 1889. There were 12 drowning deaths, and a dozen others died of heart conditions, apoplexy, exposure and other causes.

The scare was not over. When rain started falling again on the afternoon of March 18, a report circulated that a dam on the Stonycreek that was many times the size of the South Fork dam had given way. Whistles wailed, sirens sounded, and shouts were heard: "To the hills! The dam has broken!" The streets were quickly emptied, but, in fact, the dam had held.

The outside world again offered help in the massive cleanup. A contingent of 2,000 National Guardsmen, along with state and county police and 7,000 workers and 350 trucks from the Works Progress Administration were soon assisting in the work of digging out the town. Johnstowners went to work, too. They threw their energies into repairing and rebuilding, making extensive renovations in the process. The recovery gave birth to the city's sharpest business revival since the Depression.

But this time Johnstown's citizens mobilized to achieve a permanent solution to the flooding problem. About 15,000 of them wrote to President Franklin Roosevelt pleading for Federal aid to dredge the rivers. In June Roosevelt signed legislation authorizing the Government to build dams and river walls in the nation's worst flood zones. He came to Johnstown in August, toured the largely restored flood zone and told 50,000 cheering residents in Roxbury Park, "We want to keep you . . . from facing these floods again." While the Johnstowners waved banners that read "You Heard Our Plea" and "Dam Our Floods," the President pledged that the Federal Government would cooperate with the state and community to solve the problem once and for all.

The U.S. Army Corps of Engineers gouged out the first bit of mud in August 1938 for what was to be the most extensive channel improvement in American history. During the next five years, the Corps widened, deepened, and realigned 9.2 miles of channel in the city, and encased the river banks in concrete and reinforced steel. On November 27, 1943, Colonel Gilbert Van B. Wilkes, chief of the Pittsburgh Corps of Engineers district, came to Johnstown for a final inspection of the work and told a group of city leaders: "We believe that the flood troubles of Johnstown are at an end . . . . We salute the flood-free city of Johnstown."

The elated community rushed to share the good news with the outside world, hoping to bring new business to the town. In a campaign organized by the Chamber of Commerce, thousands of Johnstowners wrote to relatives and friends across the country to report that the city's floods were at an end. Mayors and corporate executives across the country received the glad tidings in a deluge of flyers. *Life* magazine and other publications pictured Johnstown's placid rivers in their new, concrete straitjackets. The Flood City chapter of the Daughters of Pythias now called themselves the Flood-Free chapter. The memory of floods was virtually purged from the community's consciousness. Newcomers to the town heard little about the tragic past.

In a 1982 article in *Pennsylvania Heritage* magazine, historian Alan Clive observed that the Corps of Engineers knew that it could not guarantee Johnstown would never have another flood, no matter what Colonel Wilkes had said in 1943. "Each project the Corps builds is designed to carry off the greatest flood of record, but records in America rarely go back more

Destruction near the Point
after the 1889 flood.

than three centuries," Clive wrote. "Nature always has another trick up its sleeve, even though it may be slow to deal out the cards."

For years what Clive called Johnstown's "submarine expressway" carried off the spring snow melts and rising river waters. When tropical storm Agnes pounded the state from east to west in June 1972, deluging Harrisburg, Wilkes-Barre and other cities and killing scores of people, Johnstown's river walls held and the city escaped with its flood-free self-image intact.

But on the night of July 19, 1977, nature played another of its tricks. As Clive described it: "A line of severe thundershowers advanced across the crest of the Alleghenies and took up position over Johnstown. Instead of moving on, the freakish storm stalled above the city, loosing blinding displays of lightning and incredible torrents of water. Rain began to fall at about 10 P.M. and continued unceasingly until 4 A.M. in the morning. The quaintly named creeks—Solomon's Run, Sam's Run, Peggy's Run, and the rest—carved new, deeper, and wider beds, smashing through expressways, apartment houses, factories, and homes." Then the water company dam broke, swept through Tanneryville and sent the waters of the Conemaugh backing up into Johnstown. The rivers rose until they approached and then exceeded the levels of the 1936 flood in some areas. They overtopped the concrete embankments and began cascading into the city.

Along with grief from the loss of lives and property, there was a sense of betrayal. The message was underlined by one resident who right after the disaster scrawled on the weathered side of City Hall, "Johnstown Is Not Flood-Free."

But for the third time in 88 years, the community threw itself into the tasks of reconstruction. Side by side, neighbors sorted through the debris and dug out the muck. "WE *WILL* REBUILD TOGETHER," announced one billboard. "A kind of Battle of Britain mentality settled in among the survivors," Clive wrote, "a sense that they had withstood the worst Nature could hurl at them and had prevailed." This flood also produced a memento that became a best-seller, a plaque picturing a donkey's hind-quarters and reading, "Flood Free Johnstown? My ---."

The damage to property was estimated at $300 million. This time after rebuilding, the shaken community took steps to lessen the danger. Studies were done that pinpointed weaknesses in the flood-control system and recommended ways to manage the flood plain more efficiently. Today the city has an extensive plan for coordinating the response to emergencies such as floods. Because storms can move into the valley with great speed, the U.S. Weather Service constantly monitors clouds in the area through a satellite and radar system and issues warnings over radio and TV when unusual amounts of rain are expected. A corps of volunteer weather spotters and automatic gauges planted at key locations report to the Weather Service on the amount of rainfall and the height of the rivers.

Fortunately, nature deals its tricks only rarely in the lifetimes of people. The waters of time would wash away all but the deepest memories of pain and loss. What remains are the stories, the legends, the small souvenirs handed down in families, the artifacts in museums.

Closing his account of the Great Flood of '89, which clearly was written some time after the event, Warren B. Thomas noted that "the

Billboard erected after the 1977 flood.

Johnstown Flood is now but a memory, recalled only in comparison with some other disaster, and naturally the younger generations have forgotten it entirely."

Richard Mayer, chairman of the Johnstown Flood Centennial, acknowledges that many people in the community aren't aware of the history of the '89 flood. "If you ask a cab driver to take you to the breast of the South Fork Dam," he says, "chances are he wouldn't know where to go. But that may be only because of the caliber of our cab drivers."

The visitor who drives into the hills to the dam site, now a National Memorial, will be rewarded with a wonderful panorama. Standing on what remains of the north end of the dam's breast, one looks over broad fields with clumps of bushes and thick evergreens, crossed by a muddy stream. With the help of National Park Service Ranger Bruce Ooton, the imagination fills in the dimensions of the lake that once filled this valley.

Farther up the hill, at the end of a quiet suburban street, are two of the "cottages" that belonged to members of the South Fork Hunting and Fishing Club. One of these Victorian dowagers is still occupied. Next to it, the red, wood-frame house with hexagon-shaped turret and twin gables that was owned by Max Moorehead, who was once president of Pittsburgh's Monongahela Navigation Co., is empty; a visitor can stand on the front porch and peek in a window.

A short way down the road stands a rickety, three-story wood building with a long porch and rows of windows. Resembling a resort hotel that has gone to seed, the structure is shut except for a bar on the main floor that sometimes gets busy on weekends and occasionally has a live band and dancing on Saturday night. Most of the time, however, its rooms are an inexpensive refuge for the homeless. This is the clubhouse where the likes of Andrew Carnegie, Andrew Mellon and Henry Clay Frick relaxed after the hard work of empire-building.

*The original club house of the South Fork
Fishing and Hunting Club. It is today the home
of the "1889 Club."*

Steelworkers at Bethlehem Steel's Lower Works
preparing to adjust housings at the nine-inch
rolling mill.

MEN OF STEEL

At the entrance to the nine-inch rolling mill in Bethlehem Steel's Gautier Division along the Little Conemaugh River adjacent to the downtown area, Jim Foster is talking to some visitors about a Congressman he saw on television. During a hearing on the steel industry, the Congressman had suggested that America's steelworkers aren't used to working very hard. This did not sit well with Jim Foster, a burly, mustachioed man who has been a steelworker for 21 years and is now a foreman. "I'd like to see him come down here and try a couple of passes in the mill," he says.

Once inside the mill, the visitors can understand what Foster means and why the Congressman might not want to accept his challenge.

The long factory building is built around a series of rolling tables placed end to end to form a horseshoe assembly. Moving along the tables one at a time, powered by a 500-horsepower drive, are glowing red steel bars, each about 20 feet long and weighing 700 pounds. At each station along the horseshoe, a worker in hard hat picks up the front of the bar with tongs and deftly places it in a groove in the stand of rolls. The bar moves through the groove, which gives it one facet of its shape, and onto the table on the other side, where it continues moving toward the next station and the next roller.

Woe to the roller whose mind is wandering and who turns to talk to one of his buddies before making sure that bar is coming out the other side!

The 700-pound bar, heated to 1800 degrees F., can jam in the roller housing and, in Jim Foster's words, "come right back in your face." Foster explains that the worker must always think in advance "which way he is going to go" if the bar bounds back at him. "You've got to be able to pack up your bags and get out fast," says Foster, whose wry way of putting things is always to the point. What happens if the roller doesn't get out fast enough? "A red-hot rod can go right through you, like a spear."

Of Bethlehem Steel's four rolling mills in the Johnstown division, two are fully automated but the other two are hand mills that still rely heavily on the skill and dexterity of human labor. The hand mills display vestiges of the steelworker's art, the excitment and dangers as well as the everyday tedium that characterized the lives of an unusual breed of men, such as Jim Foster.

The making of raw steel was also fraught with extraordinary risks and, in its early years, inspired spectacular imagery. Here is how one writer, Robert H. Walker, described the Promethean process in a book entitled *Everyday Life in the Age of Enterprise, 1865–1900*:

"The ovens dwarfed in size most man-made objects that Victorian Americans had ever seen. The heat required to produce the steel created a climate suggestive of the hellish scenes depicted by fire-and-brimstone preachers of the traveling circuit. As the air drafts were applied, enormous showers of sparks mounted to the sky, belittling any Fourth-of-July display. As a visual climax, the molten steel came tumbling out, shimmering in volcanic intensity and distorting the very air about it. In the midst of this elemental display, mysteriously goggled, his sinewy strength exaggerated by the flame of heat-reflected sweat, moved the steelworker."

The magnitude of the tasks, as well as the devotion of steelmen, inevitably gave birth to a Paul Bunyan kind of folk hero named Joe Magarac, created by the first generation of Slav steelworkers in the Monongahela Valley. Magarac, the story goes, was a a seven-foot "Hunkie" with prodigious strength, born inside a mountain, who worked day and night in the mill, feeding the open-hearth furnace, stirring the molten steel with his fingers, and shaping rails with his bare hands. When he took off his shirt, he proved to be literally made of steel:

"By Gods, he no tell lie. He was steelmans all right: all over, he was steel same lak is from open hearth, steel hands, steel body, steel everything."

Unlike Paul Bunyan, however, Magarac was no free spirit. As Robert Walker wrote in his book, Magarac—whose name in Slavish meant "jackass"—was like a beast of burden. "He was a slave to his job, and he glamourized not so much man's power as man's subservience to a process and a product." When the mill owner decides to close down Joe's furnace, the hero deliberately melts himself into a batch of steel with which he hopes his boss will build a fine new mill.

Though the steelworker was in some ways slave to the furnace, he was also its master. In *Crisis in Bethlehem,* John Strohmeyer, for many years editor of the *Globe-Times* in Bethlehem, Pennsylvania, described the blue-

Blacksmiths testing the strength of steel
at the Bethlehem Steel's Lower Works,
an historic building built 1862.

*The eleven-foot mill of the
lower works.*

collar elite who tended the open-hearth furnaces and whose skill and on-the-spot judgment was essential in making high-quality steel. The open-hearth foreman, who normally supervised five furnaces, had to be a mentally tough leader who combined the talents of platoon sergeant, band leader and master chef. Directly under him was the first helper, who was in charge of loading, maintaining and controlling the furnace. A second helper assisted the first in obtaining alloys for the heat and tapping the furnace when it was ready; according to Strohmeyer, he sometimes had to lift and move 500 pounds of manganese alloy in a wheelbarrow. Three or four brawny third helpers assisted the second helper when the tapping began or swung a sledgehammer and braved the heat when ordered to do so. All the furnace men wore long underwear the year round, to protect them against the heat in the summer and the cold in the drafty buildings during winter.

Overhead cranes deposited batches of scrap metal in the open-hearth furnaces along with ladles full of molten iron. When the liquid iron, still about 2,500 degrees F., hit other, partially melted materials already in the furnace, the mix began boiling violently. From time to time, the first helper assessed the progress of the heat through a peephole or opened the furnace door to extract samples with a long-handled spoon. The charge took about five hours to melt; to make sure the whole mass had melted, the first helper probed the depths of the furnace with a long one-inch square bar affectionately called a "Hunkie periscope."

When the mix was found wanting—specialty steel requires varied amounts of such ingredients as silicon or nickel—helpers working on the furnace floor shoveled added quantities of one or another material directly onto the furnace banks. Strohmeyer calls this "the ultimate test of steel-making stamina." The furnace men, led by the first helper, lined up in front of the door to the hearth; then, as flames leapt out at them, each moved toward the door, one after another, and "with a long and graceful swing" threw his load into the furnace, finishing with one arm and shoulder in front of his face to protect it from the flames.

In this sweat-filled, macho world, many languages were spoken and formal introductions were seldom made. The men were known by such nicknames as "Young Martin" and "Old Martin," "Shamrock," "Black Hand," "Tomahawk" and "Popeye," "Wild Bill," "Tricky Mickey," "Slim," "Fats" and "Patsy." According to Strohmeyer: "This breed of workers gave corporate 'fat cats' little respect. In fact, some of the long-time melters refused to identify with either the union or the company, claiming their own role in steelmaking was unique." Nor did they work only for money. After years of living with steelworkers and listening to them talk about their jobs, Strohmeyer was convinced that the men "were drawn to the mills because steelmaking is a rugged test of manhood and virility."

When hard times came to the American steel industry in the 1980s, the livelihoods as well as the pride of thousands of steel workers were threatened. During three decades of postwar prosperity, Big Steel and the United Steelworkers had become locked into a wasteful and extravagant dance in which the ranks of management became bloated and wages and benefits whirled constantly upward without corresponding increases in productivity. The customers were, meanwhile, beginning to demand better quality steel; with new technologies and management practices, foreign companies and smaller mills in the United States were capturing larger and larger shares of the market.

New regulations ordered by the Federal Environmental Protection Agency (EPA) in the 1970s hit Johnstown with its aging plant especially hard. Bethlehem concluded it would be simply too expensive to modernize some of the mills to meet the anti-pollution requirements, and, in 1973, announced that 4,700 jobs would be eliminated over a period of four years.

A community with a lesser tradition might have reacted with handwringing despair or angry protest. Instead, with encouragement from the steel company, the city fathers organized an association called Johnstown Area Regional Industries (JARI) and, within a year, had raised $3 million for industrial development in the area.

Impressed by the city's own efforts to diversify, Bethlehem—the major contributor to the fund—committed itself to bringing new steelmaking technologies to Johnstown. A basic oxygen furnace was nearly installed. But damage to the Bethlehem plant during the 1977 flood was heavy, and there was talk of the company pulling out. Again, the city won a reprieve from the company's top management, which had always regarded the Johnstown works with special affection because of its history and reputation (Chairman Lewis W. Foy was a Johnstown native). In 1981, the company brought two 185-ton electric-arc furnaces to the works. The modern furnaces make steel by melting scrap metal with massive jolts of electricity and eliminated many steps of integrated steelmaking such as fuel preparation in coke ovens and separation of iron from its ore in blast furnaces.

When the country slid into a recession in 1982 and steel companies began closing down plants all over the country, it looked as if Johnstown had exhausted its appeals and the death sentence would be carried out. Bethlehem closed down its furnaces in the city for nine months. At about the same time, U.S. Steel announced it would phase out its "tailor shop" in Johnstown, where for most of the century it had made equipment for the industry such as slag pots and coke oven doors. The unemployment rate in the city reached 26 percent, the highest in the country.

This time local union leaders emerged as the heroes. The battle to unionize steel plants had been long and bitter. Bethlehem, like the other big companies, had not recognized the United Steelworkers until 1941, but since then Johnstown had become a strong union town. Even bank tellers and dairymen carried USW union cards. And the local staff representative of the USW, as Strohmeyer reported, lived up to the sign on his office wall, which read: "Yea, though I walk through the valley of the shadow of death,

*A realistic bronze sculpture of a steelworker
leaning against the "Tribune-Democrat" building
in downtown Johnstown.*

I shall fear no evil, for I am the meanest son-of-a-bitch in the valley."

Nevertheless, when the company insisted on negotiating a separate agreement with the six union locals in Johnstown, as the price of keeping the mills open, the leaders went along. In long, tough negotiations, they agreed to sweeping changes in archaic work rules that would, among other things, combine some jobs and result in more layoffs. They agreed to cuts in pay, in vacations and in holidays, receiving in return promises of profit-sharing and pension increases that would pay off only in the long term. The rank-and-file members approved the pact, although they later voted all but one of the leaders out of office.

The concessions were many, and the pain in the community was widespread. But on his visits to the community Strohmeyer "heard only expressions of community pride for a union that had the courage to face realities. . . . Further, the union vote helped spread the message that Johnstown has a labor climate conducive to industry." In addition, the city fathers engineered a $22 million buyout of the U.S. Steel plant. Jack Sheehan, a manufacturer and a former Governor of the Federal Reserve, put together the financing in just 71 days in what became a model private-public partnership. With concessions from the union, the Johnstown Corporation—its new name—now employs 600 and is very profitable. In addition, Sheehan in 1988 bought Bethlehem's axle plant in the Lower Works, which had not operated for years. The reopened plant was expected to employ 60 to 70 people.

Although the city had saved what was left of its major industry for a time, there were no guarantees that Bethlehem would remain in the city. Despite a general return to profitability by the steel companies in the late 1980s, the Bar, Rod and Wire Division was still losing millions of dollars a year.

But a new era in union relations had been inaugurated in Johnstown. And Bethlehem was betting heavily that a new kind of management—and

*Blacksmith's tools hanging on a rack, creating
their own sculptural pattern which memorializes
the 129 smithies who once worked for
Bethlehem.*

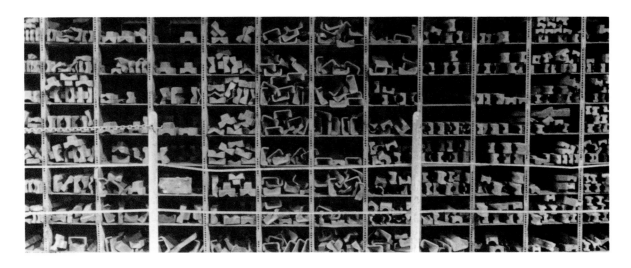

*Guides for the eleven-inch mill in Bethlehem's
Lower Works are stored in racks. The random
arrangement of these shapes creates forms
worthy of a contemporary sculptor's
creative design.*

A detail of the "sculptural forms" in the storage rack.

*Templates for machine parts which were once
used in the Bethlehem steel mills create their own
unique composition as they hang on the wall.*

a new breed of steelworker—would help turn the Johnstown operation around.

To head the Bar, Rod and Wire Division (which includes a mill in Lackawanna, New York), Bethlehem looked outside its own management ranks and brought Theodore Leja to Johnstown in 1984. Leja had run steel minimills in New York, Texas and other states. Bethlehem wanted a man like Leja with entrepreneurial talents, who was not captive to the habits of the past and could run the Johnstown division virtually as an independent business.

The ironies were many. Early Polish immigrants to Johnstown had been shut out of the skilled jobs in the mills. The man sent to save the mills in the 1980s was the son of Polish parents. He grew up in France and later in Binghamton, New York. A genial, blond, blue-eyed manager in his 50s. Leja still speaks with a slight accent. His style is a far cry from that of the old regime of the Cambria Iron Works and even the steel industry of 50 years ago.

While their routines were once dictated from above and conditioned by complex union rules, today steelworkers must be participants in a process of "continuous improvement." The division in Johnstown tailors a variety of steel products to the specific needs of their customers. Workers sit on Labor-Management Participation Teams that constantly discuss ways to improve quality and increase efficiency. Workers' ideas are no longer ignored, they are solicited. Leja even encourages them to visit steel purchasers to see first-hand how customers use the products and to hear more about their needs. The company shares information with them on their progress and on the division's financial condition. In short, Leja believes that the future of steelmaking in Johnstown depends on winning the cooperation of the workers through a team effort.

What is involved is a cultural transformation. "When we started a program to turn the division around," Leja says, "we had to improve our efficiencies and reduce our costs by harsh percentages. This was overwhelming to people. They didn't see how it could be done, because they felt they were already working hard—they were. We had to figure out how to work *differently*. And, in fact, we have made tremendous gains; our productivity has gone up by 20 to 50 percent in the last three or four years."

Many generations of Johnstowners have worked in steelmaking; a strong tradition of craftsmanship remains. If some of the macho has gone out of steel work because of the introduction of automated methods, it has been replaced by new kinds of challenges for younger workers. "This is not the kind of industry it was five years ago," Leja says. "The difficult jobs have become less physical. There is a completely different atmosphere in the plants. We offer good pay, exciting things to do, a cleaner environment. We are trying to involve workers, to increase their skills and knowledge. If we work together, pull together as a team, tremendous things can happen here. There are tremendous opportunities if people are willing to change more rapidly."

*Architectural harmonies in the roofs of
Bethlehem's Gautier Division.*

*In the early years of the twentieth century the
Park View Theater occupied this classically
inspired building on Main Street.*

A PLACE TO PLAY

When Michael Novak, a philosopher and theologian, thinks about growing up in Johnstown, he remembers the story of Babe Ruth's home run in the Point Stadium. No one had ever hit the distant right field wall in Johnstown's stadium, his father told him, until Ruth appeared there for an exhibition game. Ruth's homer cleared the wall and was still rising when it left the ballpark.

Novak, whose writings include a book on *The Joy of Sports*, also remembers "mean, tough football" played by the sons of coal miners and steelworkers. Sports rivalries were fierce in these western Pennsylvania towns, and the fans were deeply embroiled. Novak recalls that when a riot broke out at a game between the Johnstown Trojans and Altoona in the 1930s, the two high schools did not play each other again for years.

Sports metaphors spring easily to Novak's mind when he talks about his hometown. The people raised there, he says, are never surprised by adversity and always prepared to meet it. "It makes you very aware that when you're behind in the last quarter, with fourth and 10 yards for a first down, you go for it."

Johnstown is a place to play as well as work hard. Sports legends are more likely to be talked about than floods. If some of the city's entertainments are rugged, Johnstowners have also known gentler pursuits, soothing to the spirit.

The serene beauty of the hills, with its sunshine, fresh air, and wooded trails has always beckoned. In the 19th century, families mounted the West-mont hill for picnics and to watch horse races at a track that once covered 28 acres where the Cambria Works had its farm and livery stables. What is now Luzerne Street was one axis of the track, which opened in 1893. Outings for the races were always festive occasions. Between races, the spectators were treated to such spectacles as hot-air balloon launchings, chariot races, and parachute jumps.

Down in the valley, Johnstowners flocked to Luna Park, where they could ride the roller-coaster and merry-go-round, take a rowboat out on the lake, or dance on at a pavilion built on a wooded hillside. The park, which opened in about 1895, offered a variety of daytime and evening entertainments, from harness-racing to boxing matches and theatrical per-formances. During the summer months, young people jumped on open, yellow streetcars in the downtown, laughing and singing, for the short trip to Luna Park (now Roxbury Park). The amusement park owners gradually shut it down around 1920 because of financial difficulties.

Around the time of the 1889 flood, the Johnstown Reed Band was a source of pride to the community.

Though the city of Johnstown today tends to empty of people after dark and on weekends—most of the office workers withdrawing to homes in the suburbs—the downtown was for many years the place to go with the family on a Saturday night. Before the 1936 flood, 11 theaters were clustered in the central business district, most of them operated by a family named Panagotacos. The Globe, Grand, Nemo, Park View, Park, State and Strand theaters played movies; the Cambria theater featured Broadway shows, and the Majestic was a showcase for vaudeville.

According to a recent National Park Service history, the Majestic brought the likes of Houdini, Al Jolson and Eddy Cantor to perform in Johnstown, and "for a racy ending to the evening, stripteaser Sally Rand." People who came to Johnstown for a Saturday night could also hear the swinging sounds of the Big Band era; performers such as the Dorsey Brothers and Ozzie Nelson always drew a big crowd at the Auditorium ballroom. Afterwards, the hungry theatergoers gathered in popular eateries such as the Elite Candy Store and Kredel's Drugstore on Main Street.

By far the most lavish of the Panagotacos theaters was the State Theater, which was famous for its extravaganzas. Built in 1926 at a cost of $700,000, the theater featured a crystal chandelier, a $35,000 Wurlitzer

The Cambria Theater on Main Street
featured Broadway shows in the 1950s.

organ and three kinds of marble in the lobby. A Johnstown resident recalled one memorable moment during the theater's opening night:

"I was there opening night on that Fourth of July. One thing I remember: A couple danced and the girl had on a circular skirt that was very wide and the top of it was striped. Underneath, though, when she turned, it was blue with stars. I'll never forget that."

Several of the theaters were destroyed in the 1936 flood and never rebuilt. Today the State Theater is part of the Lee Hospital auditorium. The only other vestige of the theater era in Johnstown is the Embassy, formerly the Nemo. This theater on Main Street was actually a Presbyterian church that had been turned into a morgue during the 1889 flood. Panagotacos did not want to demolish the church because of its history and so built his theater facade and marquee right over it. The Embassy is now closed; a project was under way to re-expose the church facade and restore the interior.

Johnstown has always been a big sports town. Baseball in the city goes back to the post-Civil War era, during which a team from Hollidaysburg called the Juniatas once defeated the Johnstown Irons in one of the highest scoring games ever recorded, 134 to 31; every member of the winning team scored at least a dozen runs. In 1920, a team called the Johnstown Independents, strengthened by the addition of shortstop Roxey Roach and pitcher Count Hilty, defeated the Cleveland White Autos in a three-game playoff for the semi-pro baseball championship of the world. The city's entry in the Middle Atlantic League, the Johnstown Johnnies, won league championships in 1925, 1926 and 1930. During the 1930s and '40s, the Negro Baseball League played some games in Johnstown, and local fans saw three all-time greats play at the Point Stadium, Satchel Paige, Jackie Robinson and Josh Gibson.

Minor-league hockey teams have come and gone in Johnstown. The Johnstown Jets competed in a league that, according to George Fattman,

Several Johnstowners have gone on to become professional athletes: Left: *Pro Football Hall of Famer Jack Hamm;* Right: *Professional Basketball Star Pat Cummings*

editor of the *Johnstown Tribune-Democrat*, was just as bloody as the one portrayed in *Slap Shot*. The Jets were succeeded by another team, the Johnstown Red Wings, who were recruited as extras for the film starring Paul Newman. The whole town virtually became a movie set during the 1976 filming of the amiably cynical story of a small-town hockey franchise called the Charlestown Chiefs. Signs urging residents to "Please keep Charlestown clean" went up along Main Street and in Central Park. Johnstowners came to cheer the Chiefs at the Cambria County War Memorial Arena where the scenes of battle on ice took place. Fattman recalls that the Red Wings were in the playoffs of their league that year, but were so debilitated by the long hours of filming that they lost the championship and the league collapsed. Afterwards, in another example of life imitating art, a new team was formed called the Johnstown Chiefs.

All the Right Moves, the 1983 film with Tom Cruise, shows that high school football is not taken lightly in the steel towns. Though the story of a team that loses its big game to a more affluent rival school is fictional, the real pride and hope that some communities invest in the success of their high school teams is a principal theme.

People can remember when 21,000 or 22,000 fans attended Johnstown High School's games in the prewar years, according to coach Jerry Davitch. In the late 1950s, when Davitch played on an undefeated Johnstown team, some 15,000 fans turned out for games. Since then, as smaller enrollments have cut into the talent pool, the team has been in the football doldrums. But in 1988, under Davitch, Johnstown pride was back as the Trojans posted the high school's 500th victory and won their conference with an 11–1 record.

The Johnstown area has produced more than its share of athletes who have gone on to sports glory, among them Johnny Weismuller, who grew up in the small coal-mining town of Windber and was an Olympic swimmer before playing Tarzan in the movies; Jack Hamm, a linebacker on four

Johnstown girl rooting for Cy Young Award winner Pete Vuckovich before the 1982 World Series.

Pittsburgh Steelers championship team and a member of the National Football Hall of Fame; Pete Vukovich, a Cy Young award winner who pitched in a World Series for the Minnesota Twins, and Pat Cummings, who played forward for the New York Knicks and more recently the Miami Heat. The Johnstown area even claims a frisbee superstar, Don Rhodes of Hornerstown, who was declared Freestyle Frisbee Disc Champion of the World in a 1979 competition.

The local passion for sports is such that a group of younger business leaders have since 1984 been trying to promote Johnstown as the "Amateur Sports Capital of America." One of the organizers is D. C. Nokes, Jr., 34, a wiry, rapid-fire talker whose brain teems with ideas for bringing business to Johnstown. Nokes points out that the city regularly plays host in the summer to a boys' baseball competition for championship teams from around the country, the All-American Amateur Baseball Association (AAABA) Tourney. One of the biggest amateur golf tournaments is held each year at the Sunnehanna Country Club on Westmont hill. An all-star high school football game is played at the Point Stadium in June. The Johnstown Marathon is held each year in October, and an invitational basketball tournament at the War Memorial Arena in December.

Nokes, who runs a billboard and poster advertising business built by his grandfather in Johnstown, also has his hand in a few other enterprises in the city and serves on a bunch of boards of directors. A former quarterback for the Westmont Hilltop High team, he weighs not more than 150 pounds soaking wet; when he went out for football at Notre Dame, he was told to " 'come back and see the head coach tomorrow and bring your body'—I mean, they take football seriously there." After graduation, he traveled widely across the U.S. as an admissions interviewer for Notre Dame before returning to Johnstown to settle.

"When I came back here," he says, "it was a period of high unemployment in 1981–82. There were a lot of broken men and women in the community, a sense of hopelessness that starts to involve a lot of families." The Amateur Sports Capital was conceived as one modest way to lift the community's spirits at the same time as it expanded the diversions it could offer to employees of companies that might want to relocate there.

"The initiative, in my opinion, crossed all the boundaries. Buying tickets to these sports events only costs a couple of bucks, which was within the means of the unemployed as well as the affluent. The message I tried to convey was that the same attitudes necessary for success in amateur sports were present in our community, part of the fabric of our people—honesty, dedication to purpose, ability to overcome adversity. We could easily point to people who have grown up in the area who embody those qualities, who would be pretty good ambassadors for the kind of mentality we have here—people like Jack Hamm and Pete Vuckovich, Frank Kush, former coach of the Indianapolis Colts, Joe Restak, the coach of the Harvard football team, who was raised in Barnsboro."

Although Nokes' idea may not be a panacea for Johnstown's economic problems—he admits it "will never create world peace or eradicate world hunger"—sports remain part of the city's lifeblood. So do bingo and church bazaars and choral groups. Johnstown has always had a smorgasbord of pastimes for all tastes. The saloons have coexisted almost cheek-by-jowl with the opera houses. The city has had a symphony orchestra since 1929. The Southern Alleghenies Museum of Art on Main Street and the Community Arts Center of Cambria County on Menoher Boulevard have exhibits that change frequently and offer many classes and activities. A branch campus of the University of Pittsburgh, built on 635 wooded acres in suburban Richland with local contributions of money and land, also has classes and cultural events open to the public. "For the size of the community, there are a lot of things to do," says Dennis Kovach, an attorney who grew up in a town 35 miles away and now lives with his family in Westmont. "I don't think people are aware of all that's around."

*St. Casimir's Roman Catholic Church in the
Polish Parish features an array of spires and
turrets and a large rose window facing the street.*

REDISCOVERING AMERICA'S MILL TOWNS

Across America, the legendary mill towns are all, like Johnstown, struggling to find new identities. The big steel plants of the Monongahela Valley, of Aliquippa on the Ohio River, Youngstown on the Mahoning, Sparrows Point in Baltimore, Lackawanna in New York are mostly shuttered. As one journalist, John P. Hoerr, has written, "Now those giant sprawling places of enormous energy have become rusting hulks: silent and lifeless, like obsolete dreadnoughts sunk to their stacks in shallow water." Islands of light remain; some of the more modern plants were making a comeback in the '80s. But older mills were being torn down and bulldozed away.

In more cosmopolitan cities, there may be some who believe these towns are best forgotten, who view them as grim, forbidding monuments to human drudgery—"the dark, satanic mills" described by William Blake.

But inside the rusting hulks, there is much of value to be learned about the social and industrial history of the country. In a high-tech age dedicated to innovation, the engineering achievements of an earlier era are highly instructive. The skills and the achievements of the people who worked in these mills need to be more fully documented and appreciated. To visit a working steel plant is to be awed by the scale and power of the undertaking; the sight of a river of blinding-yellow molten metal gushing from its furnace into a waiting ladle is both dreadful and inspiring.

America is rediscovering its mill towns, and the mill towns are, in turn, beginning to realize the value of their heritage—and to build on it. Lowell, Massachusetts, is a model of how a once-depressed town can be tranformed by a new vision of itself. The great textile mills that encircled the city, where the factory system of production was born in America in the 19th century, had been idle for decades, ever since the textile makers began moving south in the 1920s. Economic stagnation was a way of life. Buildings of historic importance were torn down. Then, in the late 1970s, a unique plan grew out of discussions that started under the Model Cities program. The National Park Service declared downtown Lowell an urban national park. The giant shells of the mills along the Merrimack River were renovated into first-class office space and housing. The locks, canals and gatehouses of the river system that provided power to the mills were restored. Interpretive programs were developed, old trolleys and canal boats built to convey visitors to the various historic sites. Art galleries and studios were installed in the Market Mills surrounding a downtown courtyard.

Over a period of 10 years some $350 million in public and private funds were invested in a careful plan that established a preservation district and encouraged local merchants and developers to refurbish storefronts and other structures. The money came from the state, a local bond issue, bank loans and Federal funds channeled through the Lowell Historic Preservation Commission.

But the idea was not to turn the city into a museum. Although tourism has given a tremendous boost to local businesses—the city attracted 800,000 visitors in 1987—this was not just a big restoration project like the many seen in communities across the country. The planners wanted to create a more attractive environment for the residents and for companies.

The restorations have spurred the energies of the community and led to more diversified economic growth. Wang Laboratories, for example, has built a $15 million training center in Lowell, and a $22 million Hilton Hotel and conference center has gone up on the revitalized waterfront along the canal system built in the 1800s.

Dozens of towns and cities, mostly in the Northeast, have developed urban cultural parks as a springboard to future growth. Johnstown has a similar plan in mind. The National Park Service and the Johnstown Flood Museum Association have proposed several alternatives for preserving the old Cambria Iron Works and turning it into a museum of iron- and steel-making. The buildings of the Lower Works, now idle except for the black-smith and carpenter shops, are in comparatively good condition and could be renovated not only for a museum, but, as in Lowell, for other types of activities. Without a preservation plan, the present owner, Bethlehem Steel, is likely to demolish the structures to meet its own space needs.

The Park Service, as part of its Industrial Heritage Project in nine counties of Southwestern Pennsylvania, has nominated the Cambria Iron Works as a National Historic Landmark. With the approval of Congress, the Lower Works would be turned into a national urban park. The pre-liminary plans also envision the possibility of a state heritage park along the river banks, a greenbelt and pedestrian walkways that would connect the Lower Works with the Gautier Division and perhaps Bethlehem's plant in Franklin on the Little Conemaugh. The plan foresees ethnic festivals in the parks and possible re-creation of the city's streetcar line.

Though some 40 places contributed to the development of steelmak-ing in America, Johnstown is one of the few where the history can be explained as a continuum—from the early iron furnaces and forges, to the development of Bessemer steelmaking, to the modern computer-driven furnaces and rolling mills of a working steel plant—and where the various sites are relatively close to one another in a virtual showcase. Randall

*This plaque over the door of the Johnstown
Flood Museum commemorates the original
Library as well as its destruction and rebuilding,
all through the generosity of Andrew Carnegie.*

Cooley, director of the Industrial Heritage Project, cites the historically significant contributions of the Cambria Company—"an enlightened management that allowed its engineers to work on new processing techniques, the three-high rolling mill, which is still in use today, and the Kelly converter and further refinements of Bessemer steelmaking." Other elements in the story of steel are also present in Johnstown, Cooley notes, among them the importance of railroads to the industry's expansion and Cambria's success in controlling resources and industries related to steel (so-called vertical integration).

Like the Lowell preservation project, the Johnstown plan looks toward an overall urban design that would blend spaces for history, recreation and business activities. Dennis Frenchman of Lane, Frenchman and Associates, the architectural firm working on the plan, says about the strategy: "This isn't going to be a Williamsburg, a museum where time stops. The project will attempt to preserve key buildings for the story of the place—not cast the city in stone. You have to have stores, gas stations, offices. You have to weave the historical sites into the economy of the city."

Frenchman, whose firm designed the Lowell project and has planned similar urban cultural parks in New York State, Houston, Charlotte, North Carolina, and other communities, traces the roots of the approach to the nation's Bicentennial in 1976, "when people re-examined the communities they were living in and found out some interesting things." He notes that there are now about 2,500 historic districts in the United States, compared with only a scattered few about 30 years ago.

The design of an urban cultural park has to create what Frenchman calls "a strong sense of place." By that he means the structures, the layout of streets, other visual elements such as signs that interpret the history must all be arranged so that the sum total of visitors' experience "makes them feel they are in a place that's different from what they know, and that it represents something important."

*The handsomely landscaped grounds and
building of the regional office of the Metropolitan
Life Insurance Company, a commercial
landmark of present-day Johnstown.*

Before that can happen, however, the residents of the community must be convinced themselves. "If you don't renew people's sense of the city, you're fighting an uphill battle—nothing can happen. The difficulties of urban renewal in some cities have been due to just that. The community has to see the history as *the* approach to economic development. You have to get the school system, the educational groups, the ethnic societies involved. Visitors to a community pick up on the attitudes of the people who live there. So if you want others to come and live there, to invest there, you have to make the residents' attitudes a first priority."

People are often oblivious to the history all around them and its significance to others. "For years, the kids in Lowell schools were learning about the Industrial Revolution," Frenchman says, "and they never went out and looked at what they had in Lowell. It's nuts. In Johnstown, you could look at the river banks encased in concrete and say, 'My God, how awful. How can we live with this?' But I ask myself, 'How many towns have rivers encased in concrete? How can we use this to create a special sense of place?'"

The Flood Centennial was looked upon, in part, as a catalyst for future development, as a way to revive interest in the city's history, both outside the community and within it. As background for the longer-range plan, the Park Service has carried out extensive studies of the city's industrial and architectural history. "The linchpin of the project is probably an investment by the National Park Service," Frenchman says. "The Federal Government does extremely well at interpreting history, though you have to be careful or they'll sanitize it beyond belief."

Of course, an urban cultural park is not a magical solution to the problems of all Rust Belt communities. "These towns have a wealth of information on where we Americans come from, what we are capable of doing," Frenchman says. "But there is only a market for so much information. Certain towns are promoting themselves as the best place to get

157

information on certain historical themes. But there's going to be a shake-out.

"Towns that are self-aware are moving forward with this approach, those that aren't are lagging behind," Frenchman continues. As an example, he notes that Lowell "captured the market" for information about the early New England textile industry, leaving behind a city of comparable size only 10 miles away, Lawrence, Massachusetts, which had also been a textile-manufacturing center. Lawrence, he says, now seems to be putting its efforts into attracting educational institutions.

Johnstowners may be divided in their feelings about doing what is needed to bring more companies and tourism to the town. The city is handicapped by its distance from the closest major highway across the state; it is 27 miles from the Pennsylvania Turnpike. Yet many feel that Johnstown's relative isolation is what makes it a desirable place to live, and that a new east-west artery that drops off more traffic in their midst would change all that. What keeps many people in Johnstown is its small-town atmosphere, its relatively low cost of living and absence of crime. Even with the high unemployment of recent years, the city in 1987 was 16th on a list of "the 100 best places to live in America" compiled by *Money* magazine.

Without a stronger economic base, however, the city's cherished values may face further erosion. Though long-time residents are reluctant to leave, too many young people have to go elsewhere to find jobs. The population has been gradually declining, and aging. As in other cities, retail businesses in the downtown have suffered from the movement of people to the suburbs and the rise of shopping malls.

But Johnstowners have been learning to build and rebuild in the same place for more than 150 years. They not only cope, they move forward. Though the direction may not yet be clear, they will move forward again. In the 18th century, Tocqueville wrote about the American pioneer's boundless confidence amid a landscape of continual change:

"Through a singular inversion of the usual order of things, it's nature that appears to change while man stays immovable. The same man has given his name to a wilderness that none before him had traversed, has seen the first forest tree fall and the first planter's house rise in the solitude, where a community came to group itself, a village grew and to-day a vast city stretches. In the short space between death and birth he has been present at all these changes, and a thousand others have been able to do the same. In his youth he has lived among nations which no longer exist except in history. In his life-time rivers have changed their courses or diminished their flow, the very climate is other than he knew it, and all that is to him but the first step in a limitless career."

Johnstown was born amid the same frontier optimism, but the years have witnessed a maturing of the American spirit. The country long ago reached the end of its frontiers. Today, the career of no man or community is "limitless"; all are limited by worldwide economic forces not in their power to control.

The canal era lasted for only a little more than two decades but transformed a small backwoods town into a busy transportation center. Coal mining, railroads, the Cambria Iron Works unleashed powerful, creative energies in the region for a few decades, then quietly went over the hill. Big Steel, a mighty heart pumping out products that built the nation's cities and made it a world power, now seems a fading force; slowly, Johnstowners have abandoned the hope that the jobs in the mills—the good old days—will soon return.

Who can foresee what new role this valley will play in the rapidly changing America of tomorrow? Johnstown has had its day of woe and ruin, as Cambria's general manager, John Fulton, said in 1889. Surely, it will again have its day of renewed prosperity.

SOURCES

Berger, Karl, ed. *Johnstown: The Story of a Unique Valley*. Johnstown Flood Museum, Johnstown, Pennsylvania, 1984.

Brown, Sharon. "Cambria Iron Company, Johnstown, Pennsylvania." Historic Resource Study, America's Industrial Heritage Project. U.S. Department of the Interior/National Park Service. September 1987.

Clive, Alan. "The Dream of Security: Johnstown and Flood Control," in *Pennsylvania Heritage*, spring 1982.

Dickens, Charles. *American Notes*. Oxford University Press, New York, 1957.

Federal Writers' Project. "The Floods of Johnstown." Mayor's Committee, Johnstown, Pennsylvania, 1939.

Friedrich, Otto. *The End of the World: A History*. Coward, McCann & Geoghegan, New York, 1982.

Gutman, Herbert G. *Work, Culture, and Society in Industrializing America*. Knopf, New York, 1976.

Hoerr, John P. *And the Wolf Finally Came: The Decline of the American Steel Industry*. University of Pittsburgh Press, 1988.

Lingeman, Richard. *Small Town America: A Narrative History 1620–the Present*. G. P. Putnam's. New York, 1980.

McCullough, David G. *The Johnstown Flood*. Simon and Schuster, New York, 1968.

McHugh, Jeanne. *Alexander Holley and the Makers of Steel*. Johns Hopkins University Press, Baltimore, 1980.

Morawska, Ewa. *For Bread With Butter: Life-Worlds of East Central Europeans in Johnstown, Pennsylvania, 1890–1940*. Cambridge University Press, New York, 1985.

Pierson, George Wilson. *Tocqueville in America*. Abridged by Dudley C. Lunt from *Tocqueville and Beaumont in America*. Anchor Books, Doubleday, New York, 1959.

Reutter, Mark. *Sparrows Point: Making Steel— The Rise and Ruin of America's Industrial Might*. Summit Books, New York, 1988.

Shappee, Nathan Daniel. "A History of Johnstown and the Great Flood of 1889: A Study of Disaster and Rehabilitation." Unpublished Ph.D. thesis, University of Pittsburgh, 1940.

Strohmeyer, John. *Crisis in Bethlehem: Big Steel's Struggle to Survive*. Penguin Books, New York, 1986.

Walker, Robert H. *Everyday Life in the Age of Enterprise*. G.P. Putnam's, New York, 1967.

Wallace, Kim E., ed. "The Character of a Steel Mill City: Four Neighborhoods in Johnstown, PA." The Historic American Buildings Survey, National Park Service, 1989.